Working with Stained Glass

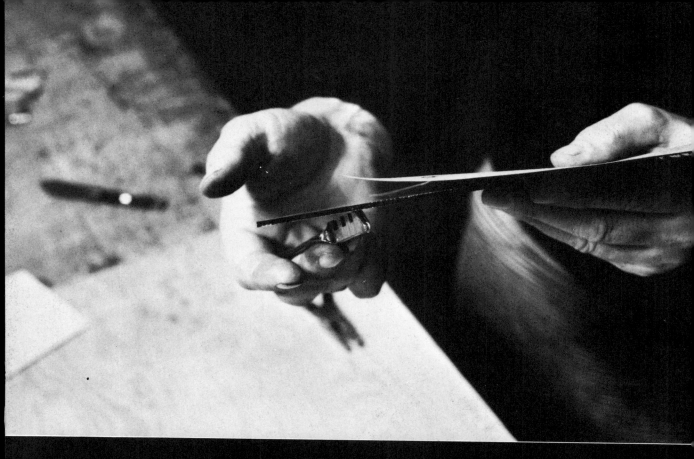

Working with Stained Glass

fundamental techniques and applications

by Jean Jacques Duval

photographs by Peter R. Stillman

Thomas Y. Crowell Company   **New York**   **Established 1834**

Designed by Judith Woracek Barry

Manufactured in the United States of America

L.C. Card 74–184975

ISBN 0-690-89706-5

2   3   4   5   6   7   8   9   10

To my son Jean-Audouin Duval with affection

Contents

ACKNOWLEDGMENTS

I first wish to thank Elga Duval for her help through the years in establishing the Duval Studio and for her organization and administration of the Duval Workshop. I also wish particularly to thank Peter Stillman for his invaluable assistance in the preparation of this book. My special gratitude goes to Judith Barry and Rosalie Brody of Thomas Y. Crowell Company. And lastly, I wish to thank all my students throughout the years who have inspired me in my own work and who helped to make this book possible.

Working with Stained Glass

Introduction

The artist lives with paradox: he would capture light but cannot. Light remains elusive, insubstantial, inimitable. He cannot paint it, sculpture it, catch it in glass. He can only use it—never truly control it.

Perhaps, however, the artist in stained glass comes closer, at his best, than do other artists; for in the finer examples of this noble and venerable form, light, medium, and subject dwell so intimately together as to become nearly synonymous and inseparable. All art, all life, is lost without light; but it is most vitally the sustenance of stained glass. For without the infinitely changing presence of natural light, the greatest expressions of stained-glass art would be dull, two-dimensional displays of craftsmanship—devices to stop the weather.

Even the earliest workers in the medium were aware of the value of light as it related uniquely to their work; and they exploited this relationship movingly. Throughout its thousand-year history, stained glass has been one of our most evocative mediums. Its emergence as a separate, important art form is coincident with the explosive growth of Christianity in Europe and the construction of the great cathedrals.

The practical necessity of providing light and protection from the elements for the vaulted cathedral interiors was adequately answered by simple clear-glass windows. The austere nature of the basic structures and the purposes to which they were put argued, however, for an offsetting brilliance; and wealthy church patrons, influenced by both exotic Byzantine religious art and the literal mode of medieval Christianity, commissioned the surrealistic marvels of light, lead, glass, and paint that have survived, in scattered instances, to this day.

Not only historically do we equate stained glass with religion. Most of us are quick to associate it with Gothic cathedrals, but even more so with the hushed silence of hometown churches and college chapels. Hence, it bears for us the personal stamp of religious devotion as well as antiquity. And to these qualities we attach those of great dignity and respectability. To catch all the related connotations of the medium within the scope of a word, we could settle on "ethereality." Indeed, even the more insouciant statements in church glass call forth sober awe when viewed from a pew. For a house of God, this is a decided plus. And a well-deserved one, we might add. For, truly, Christianity has nurtured the art.

Until relatively recently, however, stained glass was very nearly *synonymous* with Christianity, to the extent that, quite without conscious intention, organized religion imposed restraints on secular expressions in glass. That is, traditional stained-glass art has been so deeply rooted in *religious* tradition as to have resisted a parallel secular evolution. Even today, church, chapel, and synagogue art remains the largest source of commissions for most stained-glass studios.

But times are changing; and so, we believe, are connotations. New techniques, modern architectural forms, and—less measurable—changing attitudes and tastes, all have combined to move stained-glass art to a new eminence quite outside the realm of religion. Strolling through New York City's Bronx Zoo one Christmas Day not long ago, we were surprised and delighted to come upon a modern slab-glass wall in the entryway of a new building that houses nocturnal animals. The work was excellent and perfectly suited to the situation. A cocktail lounge on one of Boston's main thoroughfares provided a pleasant irony with its outside wall of brilliant *dalle* glass mounted in epoxy; for, moments before spotting it, we had concluded an inspection of some lovely traditional work in one of that city's oldest churches. The contrast was exciting—and reassuring.

Hundreds of modern office buildings, banks, schools, restaurants, hotels, civic centers of all sorts have utilized stained glass somewhere in their architecture. And not simply to let in light and keep out the weather. In contrast to the static, utilitarian leaded glass found in public buildings and private homes of 60 to 80 years ago, much of today's stained glasswork is truly art—with an architectural function.

But stained glass for amateurs? Again, unthinkable, until recently. The same individual who, spurred by the desire to express himself artistically, purchases a set of oils or watercolors on the blithe assumption that a bit of practice will lead to mastery of these hellishly frustrating mediums, would probably reject as absurd the idea of working in glass. For, after all, it does take audacity to translate into home-workshop dimensions the dramatic and often intricate work of the professional. Unless one has seen small-scale amateur work of various kinds, he has had little to inspire him and much to frighten him away.

Stained glass is an ideal medium for amateurs. To produce an attractive piece of work, be it jewelry, partition, window, lampshade, or whatever, requires less involvement than any other "legitimate" art form we can think of, and is readily teachable. We began a school on that very assumption. One of our biggest challenges, and most rewarding satisfactions, has been to prove to students of all ages and backgrounds that they can indeed accomplish fine work in glass. So can you.

Mainly, we're going to duck the question "What is stained-glass art, and what isn't?" It is closely akin to the larger pointless question "What is art, and what isn't?"—and, hopefully, better authorities than this one have ground out a large enough body of opinion on that issue to satisfy the intellectual side of your artistic curiosity.

We *will* submit that what many consider to be heretical, we consider to be delightful; and that our concern in the medium, and in this book specifically, is to provide information and excitement, using colored glass as a catalyst. If you want to construct a Tiffany-type shade, we'll show you how. Will it be art? Who cares? Tiffany didn't. What matters in the kind of alchemy that turns lead, sand, and a handful of other minerals into something breathtakingly beautiful is only the beauty itself.

We have taught hundreds of people how to work in glass, and we can count on one hand the times we have been forced to caution about a planned project: "No, you can't do that." And these few discouragements were prompted by the *technical* limitations of the medium. (With the exception of a plan for an elaborate pendant that would have weighed enough to bring its small maker to her knees.)

This is a book meant to involve you deeply in a number of forms within the medium, not to dictate narrowly the scope of your work. Our stress is on technique rather than projects. That is, we'll keep our promise about the Tiffany-type shade—but the emphasis will be on how to accomplish this kind of construction in general rather than on the building of a single, preconceived unit requiring no creative input from you. One doesn't learn much from project books, in our opinion, any more than one learns much about painting by coloring numbered diagrams. Painting with numbers requires no discipline, no inventiveness, no taste. (Infer what you will from the fact of the wide popularity of such kits.) Almost anything you tackle on the basis of what you learn in this book will, to be aesthetically pleasing, require what the number painters lack.

You may sense that our approach to the first assignment—the making of a stained-glass panel—is at odds with the somewhat freewheeling spirit suggested above. Probably so; we do try to stay particularly close to a lockstep system of instructions—and seemingly ignore the likelihood of your initial craving for creative freedom. Try to see it as a brief apprenticeship, however; we must assume your ignorance as a beginner in stained-glass crafting. Many books of this nature only pretend to consider the reader a novice, and leave maddening gaps in their instructions. Once you learn what *won't* work, we urge you fervently to try whatever *will*.

First, however, a bit about the material you will be working with.

Natural glass is as old as our planet, but it wasn't until two thousand years ago that man was able to begin to make the substance we're familiar with today. Rome had a glassmaking industry, which shifted to Constantinople along with the seat of empire. There, mostly as mosaic, colored glass was used extensively. Until the craft was established in Europe, however, glass remained relatively scarce and very costly. Despite its early use in Rome, stained glass came to Europe via the Byzantine civilization, with missionaries from the East. The Eastern influence remained strong into the Middle Ages. As the seat of the Church, Constantinople was also the source of ecclesiastical art forms. When the walled city fell to the infidels, its influence remained; the returning crusaders, excited by the exotic uses of color and form in Eastern churches, urged similar expressions in Western edifices. Those early examples of stained-glass art which remain to us for study show clearly in their portraiture a strong non-Western influence.

Stained glassmaking hasn't changed much in the last thousand years. While there have been some refinements in the process, glassmakers today follow essentially the same steps as did their counterparts centuries ago. Not all glass is handmade, of course; but the best stained glass continues to come from small factories employing highly trained artisans.

Most stained glass comes from four countries: France, West Germany, England, and the United States. No one country makes the best. Period. There are differences in thickness from country to country, and a few variations in color characteristics; but most of these are noticeable only to the professional. Normally, glass is not ordered by country of origin but by color and texture.

Glassmakers invest their product with a signature of sorts—a characteristic irregularity or distinctive feature that marks every piece. Thus, it is likely that the pattern of ripples, veining, waves, bubbles, or flecking in a sheet is not unique to that piece but is instead the "trademark" of the maker. These features do more than identify; they bring character and beauty to the glass. Each "imperfection" responds to light in a different way. As you become more familiar with stained glass, you will increasingly appreciate the value of these seeming flaws.

Glass is a product of minerals, not miracles. Yet we can with justice describe the glassmaking process as an art, quite apart from the purposes to which it is put. (We're not referring to manufactured glass as art, mind you, any more than we would refer to a backyard plaster Madonna that way.) Having honored the process, let us now describe it—in very simplified fashion.

The chance that you will attempt to make your own stained glass is remote. The skills and equipment necessary to produce even lumpy, primitive-looking glass are beyond you and your home workshop. Even accomplished artists rarely attempt it; for the process is not central to their function, any more than is the making of oil paints to the modern painter. The process *is* interesting, however—and, furthermore, adds to one's appreciation of an admirable craft.

Iron-free silica sand is the basic ingredient in fine glass. To this is added soda ash, potash, and lime. These ingredients, mixed in proper ratios and fired to temperatures up to 3,000 degrees F., will yield high-quality *clear* glass. Color is introduced into the mixture with the addition of various metallic oxides.

Under this extreme heat, the mixture fuses into a molten mass. The glassblower then gathers a blob from the clay melting pot on the tip of the blowpipe. While he forces air into the blob, he swings the pipe in a controlled rotation to keep the hollow, elongating sphere he is forming from collapsing. The cylinder, when about three feet long and approximately fourteen inches in diameter, is snipped off the pipe. It is roughly bottle-shaped, narrowing to a neck at the point nearest the pipe and less acutely at the far end. The narrower tip is sheared off, as is the bottom of the piece, and then annealed. Then the cylinder is cut lengthwise down one side and placed in an annealing oven, to gradually unroll, flatten, and cool by stages. We call the end product of this process *antique glass*. This is the glass used in traditional stained-glass paneling. It, or its machine-made imitations, is what you will use, at least at first.

Flashed glass is not basically different from antique glass, although it does have a distinctive feature. Flashed glass is laminated. When the molten blob of glass is removed from the pot, it is quickly dipped into another molten mix of a different color, then blown into cylindrical form. The result is more than the sum of its parts. Because the two colors have not actually mixed, but are instead sandwiched together, they remain distinct in tone and value. But because light travels through them both, an additional depth and coloration are achieved.

Marine antique isn't antique at all, in the technical sense of the term. It isn't blown but is rolled out by machine process. It is pretty enough and is widely used with good results; but it lacks the character of true antique, being without the irregularities that bring beauty and depth.

Cathedral glass is also machine-made, commercial glass. Slightly rougher than marine, it is otherwise the same. (We're not sneering at either type, by the way; we simply prefer blown glass to the commercial types.)

Opalescent glass is also commercial. This is the wavy-patterned, nearly opaque material used in Tiffany, and imitation Tiffany, work. It originated in the United States and is quite popular here, not only for lampshades but also for paneling.

Dalle de verre, or *slab glass*, is considerably different from the materials described thus far. Should your interest in our craft endure, you will almost certainly want to work with this alluring substance. Slab glass is handmade, but is not blown into cylinders. Instead, it is molded in flat dalles, approximately an inch thick and eight inches square. Unlike antique glass, which

These workers at the Mittinger Glass Works in West Germany are putting pots of raw materials into the oven. (Courtesy Heide Bitter)

The glass is blown into an elongated bottle shape, which will eventually be cut and flattened into a sheet. (Courtesy Heide Bitter)

The top and bottom ends of the glass cylinder are cut off in this operation. (Courtesy Heide Bitter)

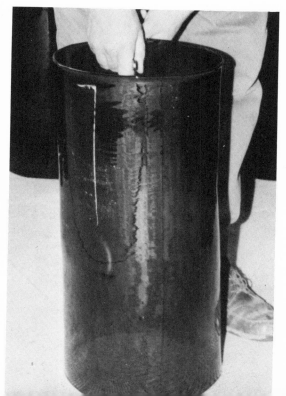

Finally, the cylinder is split before being placed in the annealing oven. (Courtesy Heide Bitter)

yields to the hand cutter, these slabs require a rather difficult cutting tech-nique—actually, more a matter of skilled breaking than of cutting.

This glass has other characteristics, however, that make it appealing to the craftsman—even the amateur. Its color is uniform, deep, and true. Its very intensity creates illusions of great depth and shimmering mystery. Further-more, its resistance to all but the crudest kind of cutting and shaping is its most positive, compelling feature. When set in either concrete or epoxy resin, its raw edges, faceted surfaces, and chunky thickness create a brute, muscular beauty. Classified as a "modern" form, this kind of glasswork is strongly suggestive of mosaic art—the very first medium to employ any kind of true glass. Slab glass differs from mosaicwork, however, in that it is transparent.

We hope you are excited already about stained glass. Most artists are, and that includes those of the first rank—Chagall, Matisse, Léger, Shahn, for example. Like any art form, this one needs a constant supply of new energies, new talent, and new ideas. We do not think it naive to entertain the hope that your excitement will endure and grow apace with your skill in the medium. Therefore, we don't address you as hobbyist but as artist (despite our sometimes oppressive instructions). Stay with us just long enough to master basics. Then, break the rules, throw the book away, create.

But don't be satisfied with beautiful accidents. We don't wish to be perverse in offering this warning. The observation of a colleague, however, needs retelling here. The real challenge to the artist in glass, he says, is not only to create beauty from manmade materials but, even more, not to be de-luded by its inherently sensational and dramatic properties. Think about that for a minute.

Tools and Materials

Virtually every craft requires an initial investment in specialized tools and equipment. The beginner, eager to make the learning process as simple and efficient as possible, often buys blindly and copiously from stained-glass suppliers' suggested lists—only to find that he rarely has use for much of what he has purchased. Just as often, one's interest in a craft is discouraged by misinformation about how much he will have to spend on basic items.

Stained-glass crafting, like many other pursuits, can be as expensive as one wants to make it. Our assumption, however, is that your interest is tempered with caution at this point—that you would rather not invest heavily on the basis of what may be no more than a whim. Thus, while we can reasonably recommend the purchase of a pair of specially designed shears (50 dollars), we are more inclined to suggest a 25-cent substitute: two single-edge razor blades. When and if you turn your skills to profit, buy the best. Until then, what follows here is a basic list that will serve nicely for traditional (leaded) glasswork. When we talk about other techniques, we will tell you of some additional necessary tools and materials.

BASIC TOOLS

1. Soldering iron. (Available in hardware stores.) This is an absolutely essential tool. We recommend a 200-watt iron for maximum efficiency, but a 100-watt model will serve adequately. Both operate on 110 volts. Don't:

    (a) buy a cheap iron. They don't heat evenly, won't last, and won't make good joints.

    (b) buy a soldering *gun*. They are not suited to the work, for a variety of reasons.

    (c) buy an iron with too large or too small a tip. Either is difficult to use—the former because it gets in the way, especially in working with small joints and seams and in jewelry; the latter because it won't spread heat quickly enough. A tip with a diameter of 3/8 inch will be suitable for most jobs. You can vary this, depending on your own ambitions.

A good iron costs between 12 and 14 dollars. With minimal care it will last for years (and is a handy household tool as well).

2. Glass cutter. (Fletcher 06 or Red Devil, available in hardware stores.) Another essential tool, the cutter is delightfully cheap. You can buy a good one for about a dollar. When it gets dull, sharpen it; after you've sharpened it a few times, throw it away and buy another. Handles and cutter heads vary somewhat in shape and size from manufacturer to manufacturer. Buy the one that feels most comfortable in your hand. (Or splurge and buy two, of different shapes.) Between projects, leave the cutter immersed in kerosene. This keeps it well lubricated.

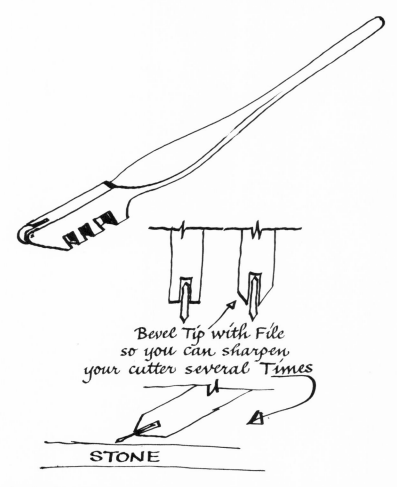

Bevel Tip with File
so you can sharpen
your cutter several Times

STONE

3. Glazing knife. (Available from stained-glass equipment houses or a local stained-glass studio, if you want the real thing.) You will need a knife of some kind for performing a number of operations. Many stained-glass craftsmen fashion theirs from cutting tools designed for other purposes. But you may not know at this point the characteristics—size, cutting edge, shape of handle—that are best for you. The basic knife will certainly serve you well, and costs only three to five dollars. (Perhaps you have already decided from the sketch that a linoleum knife will do. You're wrong; the glazing knife is sharpened along the top edge, the lino knife along the inside of the crescent.)

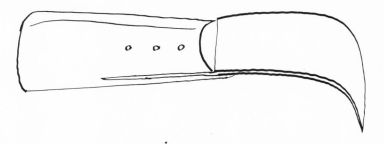

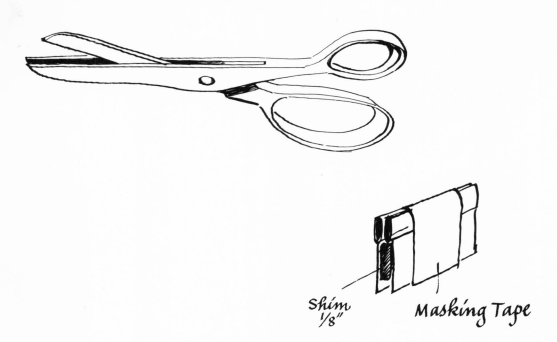

Shim 1/8" *Masking Tape*

4. Shears. (Available from supply houses or, possibly, a local stained-glass studio.) You *do* need a device that will make a 1/8-inch-wide cut in heavy kraft paper rather than a standard, thickness-of-the-blade scissor cut. You don't, however, need high-quality, precision-machined shears (from 15 to 50 dollars). Buy a packet of single-edge razor blades instead. Insert a 1/8-inch shim of wood or cardboard between them, and tape them together with masking tape. The shears may be easier to use—but not much.

5. Grozing pliers. (Available from supply houses or, possibly, a studio.) Another tool basic to many operations, grozing pliers (or *grozer*) are relatively small, with flush, smooth, narrow jaws. If we have just described an implement already in your toolbox, you don't need grozing pliers. Make certain, though, that the jaws of your pliers meet firmly and smoothly, with a fairly short bite and no lateral play.

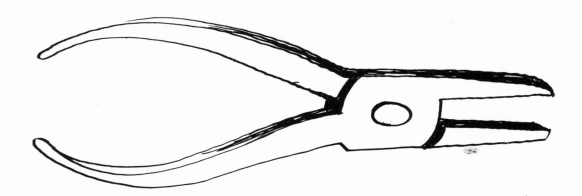

6. Hammer. (Available in most hardware stores.) Special hammers are available to the glazier at moderate price. From your local hardware store you can obtain a tool that approximates the ones in the supply house catalogs and will probably cost even less. A small to medium tacking hammer will do splendidly. Just be sure it's a good one, without too large or heavy a head, and double-ended rather than clawed.

7. Lead vise (stretcher). (Available from supply houses.) You could use the vise on your workbench instead of purchasing this little tool. Almost any vise (except wood or pipe vises) will serve to hold the lead strip for stretching purposes. The lead vise does it best, though, costs very little, and is recommended.

8. Stopping knife. Used for straightening out lead, any blunt-edged knife, such as an oyster knife, will do.

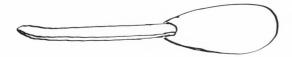

9. Lathekin. Strictly a homemade item, this tool is fashioned from hardwood to the maker's dimensions, and should be large enough to open the channels in the lead. For instance, a 3/8-inch dowel with a blunt point, the length of a pencil, will do nicely.

(The rest of our basic tools list consists of items of a nonspecialized nature. You can find them locally without difficulty and may have some of them on hand already.)

10. Matte knife. (Available at art and drafting supply stores.) Any good matte knife will do.

11. Bench brush and dustpan.

12. Scrub brush. A long, modified-figure-eight brush is best. Get a good one, with close bristles at least an inch long.

13. Drafting supplies. T-square, right angle, straightedge (at least 18 inches, calibrated in thirty-seconds), compass, pushpins, masking tape (1/2 inch), grease pencil, 4-H and H-B pencils, black felt-tip pen.

14. Drawing board. Plywood will do, but is soft and splintery at the edges. A good drawing board doesn't cost that much. It should be fairly large—about 30 x 30 inches.

15. Workboard. You *can* use the same board for drawing and glazing, but the latter involves operations which will eventually ruin it for drafting. Plywood works fine as a workboard.

16. Sharpening stone. A small oilstone will keep your knife sharp enough to perform its various jobs.

BASIC MATERIALS

1. Glass. (Available from glass supply houses or from a local stained-glass studio.) You may be able to turn up a well-supplied studio willing to do business in glass, but if you don't live in or near a fairly large city, plan to buy your glass by mail. The suppliers we have listed in the appendix are reliable and have substantial inventories on hand. Furthermore, they are willing to ship small orders—even packages of scrap—promptly. After you place a couple of orders, you will be better able to determine what kinds of glass you want, of course; but even the first time you will probably be reasonably happy with your selection.

Stained glass is more expensive than window glass, for good reason. And, in common with most purchasing, the more one buys at a time, the less the material costs. Even if you purchase in very small quantities, however, you will find that stained-glass paneling works out to a cost of from 4 to 6 dollars a square foot—really not a staggering figure, inasmuch as it includes the cost of all materials consumed, not just the glass. (Glass varies widely in cost, depending mostly on how it was made.)

2. Lead. (Most craftsmen call lead *came;* we'll call it lead.) (Available from supply houses or a studio, or by mail.) Lead comes in a variety of shapes, sizes, and textures. Don't give in to the urge to buy a little of each—at least, not at this point. We suggest that for your first work, a panel of modest dimensions and complexity, you use 3/8-inch and 1/4-inch flat lead. Buy more than your design calls for; you will surely ruin 10 to 25 percent of it before you have mastered its handling.

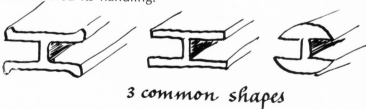

3 common shapes

3. Solder. (Some hardware stores carry the right kind. Otherwise, supply houses or a studio.) Use no-core solder. Don't let your local hardware dealer tell you that core solder will do. It won't. The 60-percent tin, 40-percent lead solder is ideal. A small spool of solder costs only about a dollar and a half and lasts a surprisingly long time.

4. Oleic acid (flux). (May be stocked by large hardware stores, but unlikely. You will probably have to order it from supply houses.) To make firm, smooth solder joints one must use flux, and the best kind to use is oleic acid. Applied lightly by brush to the intended joint before soldering, the oleic acid flows the solder, disperses the heat evenly, and helps to create a solid, attractive joint. (You may forget to use it a couple of times and will be puzzled by the porous, ugly lump that forms under your iron.) A moderately priced paintbrush no more than half an inch wide is the best way to apply the acid.

5. Glazing putty. (Any hardware store.) Even if your work won't be exposed to the weather, it should be puttied. Putty provides insulation between lead and glass, makes the construction sound and rattlefree, and adds to the neatness of the finished piece. For panels with a purely decorative function, you can get away with puttying one side; but if you mount your creation in an outside wall, putty both sides.

6. Whitening. (Most paint stores.) The flux and putty will leave a gummy residue on your work. To clean the panel, use this powdery substance, brushing vigorously across the surface with your scrub brush. A number of materials will serve in lieu of whitening, including plaster of paris.

7. Nails. You will need three or four dozen 1-inch blued nails.

8. Lath strips. (Any lumberyard.) At the beginning, 10 to 12 feet of 1/4 x 1-1/2-inch lath will do.

9. Kraft paper, drawing paper, and carbon paper. (Art or drafting supply shops.) You can buy paper by the roll or by the yard. We suggest the latter; you won't be using that much at first. Start with approximately two square yards of each of the following: lightweight drawing paper, 30-pound kraft, 80- or 90-pound kraft, heavyweight carbon paper (or typewriter carbon will do). Pick up a sketch pad at the same time; you will need it for initial designing.

THE WORK AREA

Ideally, the stained-glass craftsman has access to a large, well-lighted studio with ample ventilation, large windows, hardwood floors, a high ceiling, plenty of electrical outlets, provision for equipment and tool storage, a large drafting table, glass racks, and a couple of specially designed workbenches. If this isn't descriptive of your shop, don't despair; neither does it describe the workshops of the greatest medieval stained-glass artists.

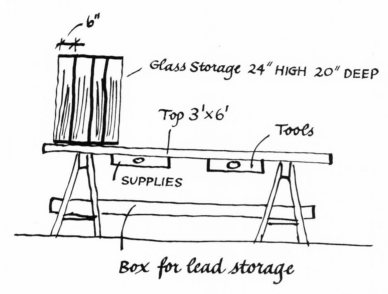

A small corner of your basement will do—just so long as it is dry and well-lighted, with an electrical outlet or two and space for a work table. Fluorescent lighting is preferable to incandescent (and sunlight vastly preferable to either). You should have a tool board within easy reach and a cabinet for storing materials. Most important, since you are going to spend hours at a time on your work, take pains to make your work area comfortable, uncluttered, and attractive. Useful custom touches are a storage bin for stacking glass and a box for lead.

Working with Leaded Glass

We are first going to show you how to make a single leaded stained-glass panel. You may not want to make a panel—but when you have completed this first work, you will have duplicated, more or less, every step in the evolution of traditional stained-glass crafting since it was first accomplished. In other words, you will have compressed a thousand years of craftsmanship into one project. And we firmly believe that you must practice these basic techniques before launching into specialized and/or "modern" departures.

Not that what we will describe is meant to be mere drill. You will enjoy the work, and the end product will probably be quite handsome. Bear with us, then. And please don't let our interruptions and seeming longwindedness throw you. We're trying to anticipate mistakes and make the instructions absolutely foolproof. Read them all the way through before starting.

THE SKETCH

You begin with a sketch. You're not going to paint figures on the glass in this panel, so the colors of the glass and the dark lines of lead are the only means of expressing your design. Keep this in mind while you consider how you want the finished work to look—what you want it to "say" and where you intend to mount it. Keep in mind, too, that you want to minimize frustration. Therefore, your design should be fairly simple and your intended dimensions modest.

We recommend a square or rectangular panel. A good working size is 12 x 12 inches, although you can double it if you wish—or stretch the dimensions to make an approximately 2-foot-square area. That's plenty for a beginner.

Of course, you may have a special installation in mind, requiring predetermined measurements. Fine, provided that you are able to translate our instructions readily to your needs. If your intended construction is much larger in area than 2 square feet and/or is irregular in its outside dimensions, don't tackle it yet. Work through a uniform panel instead and you will learn enough to make a more complicated piece.

Rule off a few rectangular areas on a sheet of drawing paper. They shouldn't be to scale at this point, for you probably haven't determined yet what shape or size you want for the finished work.

Close your eyes. Conjure, create, design in your mind's eye. Imagine sunlight transfused through a small panel of rich, glowing colored glass. Picture the dark, bold tracery of the lead forming exciting patterns, punctuating the flow of color and texture. Determine the tonal qualities you desire—muted blues, greens, and purples; flaming reds and oranges; subtle browns, mauves, grays.

Now sketch. Use a drawing pencil, medium hard. Your lines will represent the leadwork—not in actual thickness but in rough placement. Do a number of sketches within the marked-off rectangles until you hit on one, or on a combination of elements, that pleases.

Before you translate your rough sketch into a full working design, take two possibilities into account:

(1) Lead is functional as well as artistic in purpose. If you have not considered its structural aspect, you may have left large pieces of glass unsupported. In a panel of this size, lateral and horizontal support isn't necessarily critical, but for now let's assume that it is.

(2) Almost certainly you have sketched yourself into a jam. You can't be expected to know yet the limitations imposed on the craftsman by his materials. Therefore, you have probably worked into your sketch an impossible cut or a weak joint. The pictures here illustrate what will and what won't work. Study them long enough to generalize for yourself the reasons

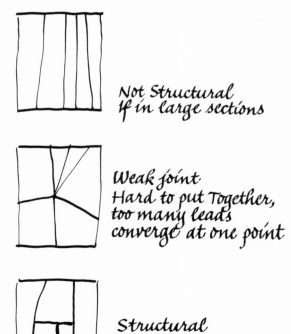

Not Structural
If in large sections

Weak joint
Hard to put Together,
too many leads
converge at one point

Structural

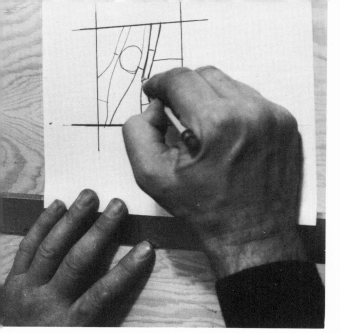

A scaled sketch layout. Here the original lines are being thickened to represent the lead.

The completed scaled sketch.

why. Then alter your sketch if necessary. (If you work only on small panels it really isn't critical, but for larger panels it is.)

If your pencil sketch now meets requirements—and is still pleasing to you—do it over to scale and then go over the lines with a black felt-tip pen. This brings you one step closer to the actual design, for the ink suggests the dark outline of the lead. (You can vary the interior widths of the lead, if taste dictates and supplies allow.) Now you are ready to color the sketch.

Watercolors give the nearest approximation to colored glass, but crayons or colored pencils will do. While this will yield no more than a vague suggestion of the finished panel, it does bring you closer to a true visualization, and also establishes a color key.

Watercolors are used for close approximation of the desired colors.

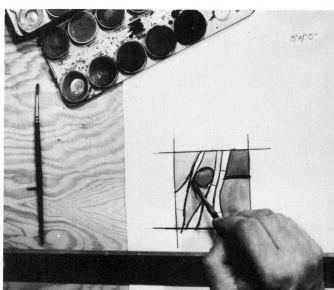

MAKING THE CARTOON

The full-sized drawing which will serve for actual patterning is called a *cartoon*. Once your sketch is done and the actual dimensions of the panel are determined, you can proceed to this step. Use lightweight (30-pound) paper, cutting it about two inches larger all around than the intended piece. Fasten it with bits of masking tape to your drawing board. Now stop—and read the next instructions carefully.

The outside borders of your panel will be formed from lead. You have already noticed that the lead is shaped like an I-beam (or an H tipped on its side). The middle part is called the *heart;* and the glass, as you can see, fits neatly into the lead channels and abuts the heart.

Simple enough, from a structural point of view. The lead holds the glass in place within its channels; the heart provides a thin wall between the interlocked pieces of glass. (The thickness of the heart doesn't vary appreciably, regardless of how wide the lead is.)

The complication arises when one forgets that the overall dimensions of the panel include the width of the outside, unused channel of the border lead. We suggest using 3/8-inch lead for the borders. This means that the *full size* of the pattern will be 3/16 inch wider on all borders than the *cut size* (the actual dimensions of the glass). In other words, half the width of the border lead lies outside the picture.

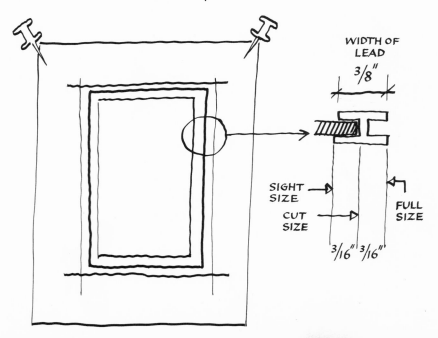

Freehand enlargement of the sketch to full-size
cartoon.

Perhaps we make too much of this obvious fact. Many novices overlook it,
however, and end up with panels that exceed the intended dimensions by
3/8 inch on both height and width. If you thoroughly understand why, you
won't make the same mistake.

In the cartoon, allow for the difference between *full size* and *cut size* by
first drawing full-size dimensions and then measuring in 3/16 inch for the
cut size (or half the width of whatever size of border lead you use). Use
T-square and straightedge for this job. Your dimensions should be exact.

Now transfer your design from rough sketch to finished cartoon. Use a
medium-hard pencil again and go lightly at first. It's a freehand operation;
you may botch it and have to erase. Be content with a cartoon that approximates your sketch. The copy job needn't be perfect. Fill in the light pencil
lines now with a felt-tip pen.

MAKING THE PATTERN

Remove the cartoon from the board, and cut a piece of 30-pound kraft and
a piece of 80- or 90-pound kraft to the same dimensions as the cartoon sheet.
Place the heavy paper on the board first. Overlay it with carbon paper cut

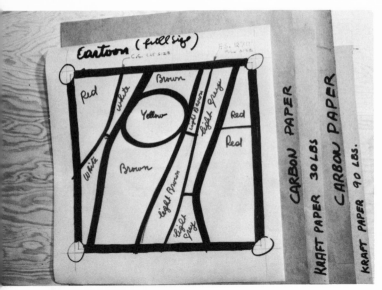

Cartoon, working drawing, and pattern in place, ready for transfer of the design.

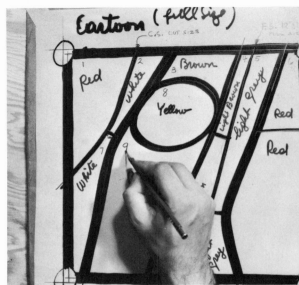

Keying each piece.

to cover the whole area. Next comes the lighter kraft paper. Overlay that with another piece of carbon paper. The cartoon goes on top. Make sure the five pieces are square with one another (and that the carbon paper is face down), and nail the stack to the board with pushpins.

Now trace the design with a 4-H pencil. Press hard; you're trying to make two clean copies. Be sure that you have missed no lines.

Next, number every piece in the design. Use any system that occurs, so long as each element is coded distinctly from the others. If the design is complex, involving many pieces, number from left to right or from top to bottom—any way that is consistent and easy to read.

Checking each piece for a strong, clear impression.

You can, if you wish, color-key the pattern too—just in case the original sketch gets misplaced or you have since changed your mind. *Y* for yellow, *Grn* for green, etc., is an easily translatable code.

This concludes the pattern-making step; but before you remove the stack from your board, remove the bottom pushpins and take a peek to be sure that the lines and codes are clear and complete all the way through.

CUTTING THE PATTERN

You can place the carbon paper and drawing board back in storage and temporarily put aside the cartoon and the lightweight working drawing. For the cutting step you will need your workboard, straightedge, matte knife, and pattern shears (or the double razor blade device we described earlier). You will also need the pattern copy—the heavyweight one on the bottom.

Carbon paper is now removed and the copies separated.

Reducing the pattern to cut size, using matte knife and straightedge.

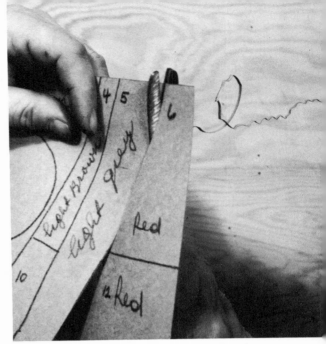

Cutting up the design with double-edge shears. Notice the filigree of paper which represents the heart of the lead.

Cutting the design with a homemade razor-blade cutting device instead of double-edge shears.

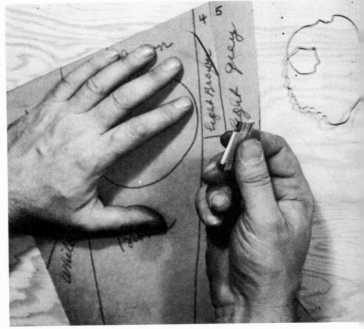

With straightedge and matte knife, cut away the margins of the pattern copy right down to the cut-size line. The next step involves either shears or razor cutter. Cut one pattern piece at a time, straddling the lines with your cutting

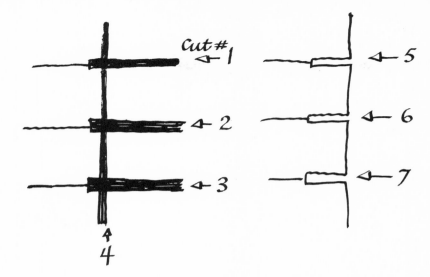

tool. The filigree of paper that falls away represents the heart of the lead, of course. If you used ordinary scissors, you wouldn't be able to make allowance for the heart; and your construction wouldn't work out.

Notice in the accompanying sketch that when you cut out a piece from the pattern, you extend the cut beyond the piece you are cutting. This will ensure that when you begin cutting the adjoining piece, you will start on the same course. If you don't extend the cut, you run the risk of misfit pieces.

Tape the cartoon to the workboard. When you have completed cutting the pattern, reassemble the pieces on the cartoon—rather like putting together

Placing the cut pieces of the pattern on the cartoon.

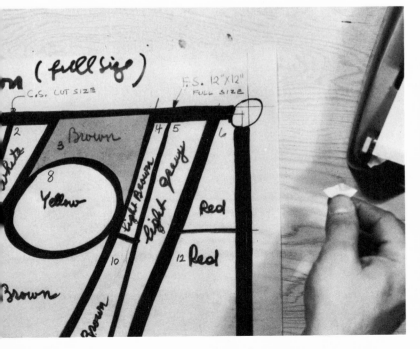
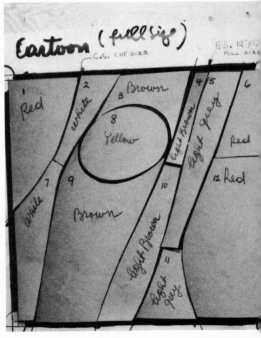

a jigsaw puzzle, with one distinct advantage: the cartoon provides the complete, keyed picture. This reassembly will establish that you haven't lost any pattern pieces.

Then fasten each pattern piece to the matching section of the cartoon, using rubber cement, temporary spray adhesive, pushpins, or loops of tape. The preliminaries are nearly over.

CUTTING THE GLASS

Roll up your sleeves. You are about to accomplish the nearly impossible. But before you start on the real thing, practice cutting something cheaper, like window glass. While it won't offer all the cutting challenges of antique glass, it will serve as a warmup and confidence-builder. Peel off a piece from the pattern. Place the glass flat on the workbench and put the pattern piece on the glass—not under it. Before you begin your first cut, position the piece to take advantage of the dimensions of the glass. It makes no sense to take a bite out of the middle of the sheet. Start from the edge, and leave a margin of glass—a minimum of 1/2 inch—around the pattern piece.

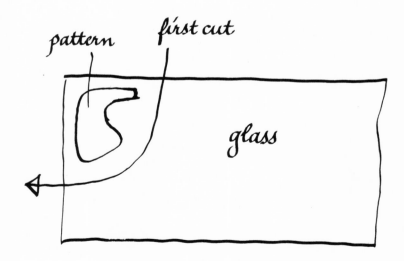

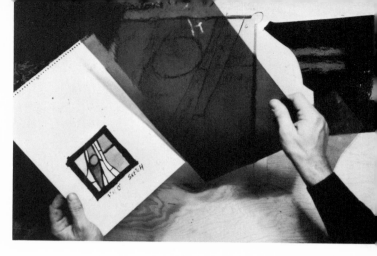

Selecting colors.

One doesn't really "cut" glass. It's too hard. Everyone knows that. What one does is to *score,* or scratch, the glass, thereby weakening it along the line. When sharp, even pressure is applied on both sides of the score, the glass should break cleanly along the line. *Snap*—a crisp, gratifying sound. It won't happen the first time.

One can tell whether or not the score is good by listening as it is made. Listen for a uniform scratching, rasping sound. Feel for resistance from the cutter as it scores. The sound and the resistance are caused by the cutter making a series of tiny digs in the surface of the glass. The score will look like a uniform scratch in the surface.

To ensure that the glass breaks evenly along the intended line, one often has to tap cleanly along the underside of the glass, following closely the course of the score. (Window glass and thin, untextured stained glass don't really need tapping; they'll snap with light pressure.) The tapping should be smart and sharp but never heavy-handed, beginning at the far edge and working toward the middle. The cutter head works best. Tap rhythmically, firmly, accurately on the underside. If you look closely, you will notice an internal fracture developing under the line. You're winning; now the glass wants to break.

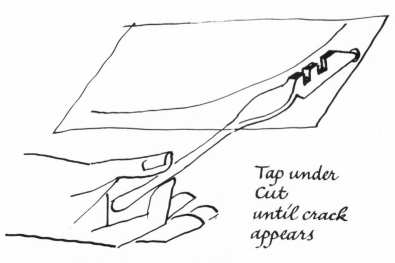

Tap under Cut until crack appears

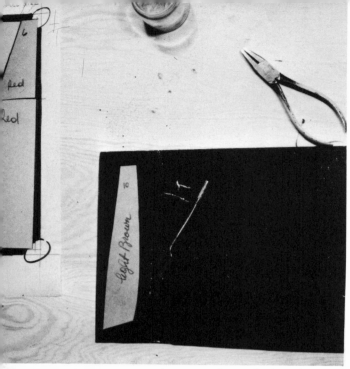

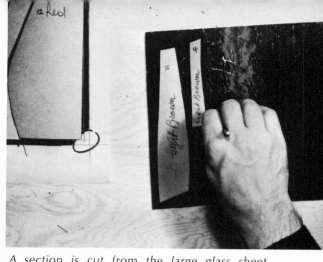

A section is cut from the large glass sheet, leaving enough margin to cut around the pattern pieces.

A pattern piece is laid on the glass.

Two ways of breaking off the section from the main sheet: applying equal pressure with each hand; and employing the table edge and a sharp downward pressure with one hand.

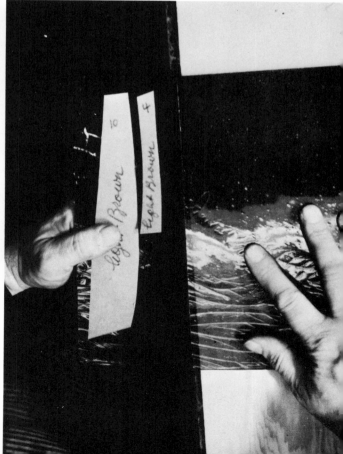

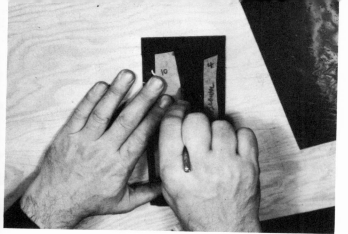

Cutting the first piece. Pattern is held firmly in place.

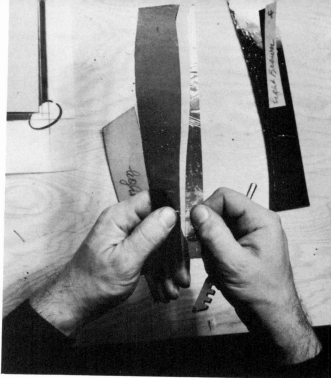

Snapping off the margin of glass. If the margin is much narrower than that shown here, grozing pliers will have to be used instead of hand pressure.

Positioning the pattern piece for the next cut.

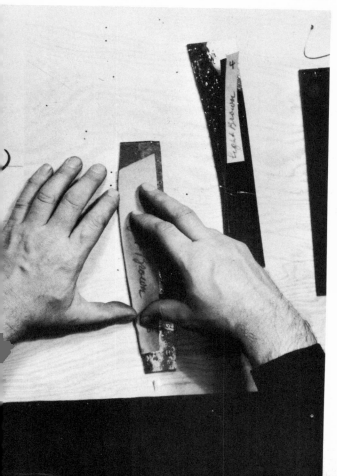

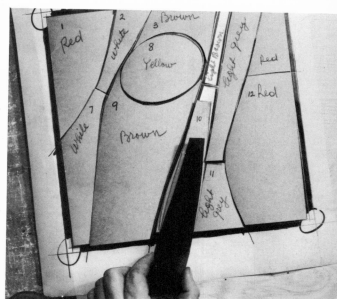

Pattern piece and matching glass are placed on the cartoon.

Dulling the fresh-cut edge by scraping with another piece of glass.

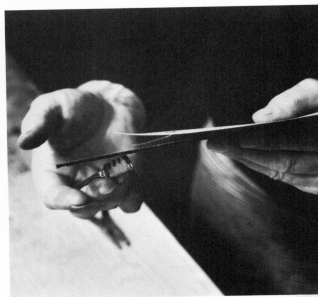

The tapping operation, seen from above and below. Look closely at the position of the cutter in the hand.

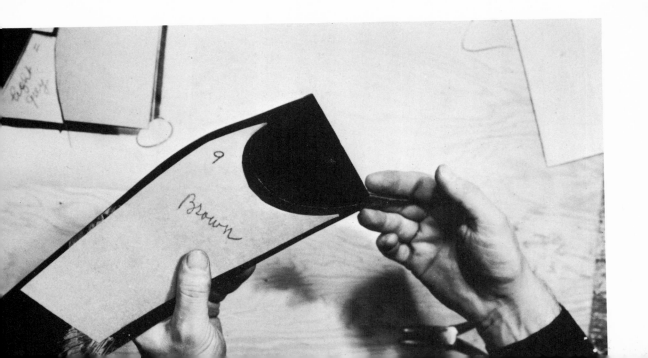

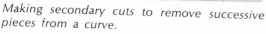

Making secondary cuts to remove successive pieces from a curve.

Breaking off the sharp points with grozing pliers.

Caution at this point: you can do such a good job tapping (particularly with thin glass) that the glass will break before you expect it to. It is remarkably frustrating to watch the glass part cleanly just where you intend it to—and then go crashing to the floor. Don't try to catch it; let it fall. And don't be discouraged. If you confine the cutting operation to the bench area, you won't lose any glass from premature parting.

In all likelihood, the first time you attempt a cut, you will fail miserably. The cutter will feel awkward in your grip; despite your best efforts, it will go skittering out of control over the steely surface of the glass; you will find yourself impossibly contorted as you try to cut around a curve; and, as perspiration forms, you will be convinced that no mere mortal, equipped with a puny, dollar tool, can make any impression on this otherwise fragile substance.

The cutting process, while initially frustrating in the extreme, is really very easy. Within the course of an afternoon's practice, you will be amazed at your increased skill. Stick to it and you will be a master cutter in no time. It doesn't take a lot of muscle, by the way. We know of one six-year-old who's a whiz.

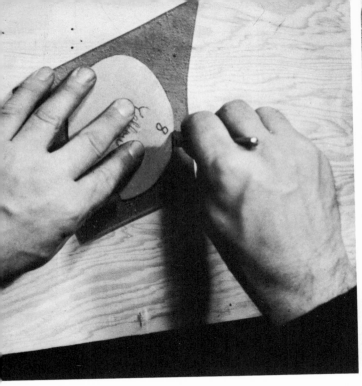
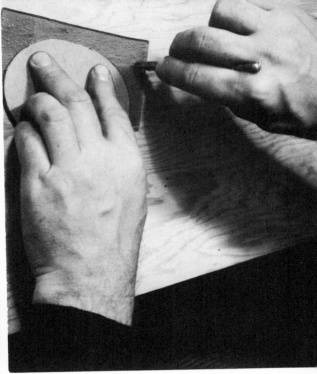

Successive stages in cutting a circular piece. Notice that pieces are removed in segments and then sharp corners are grozed away.

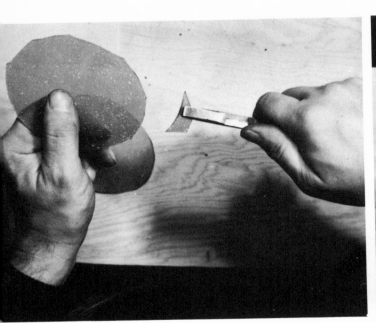
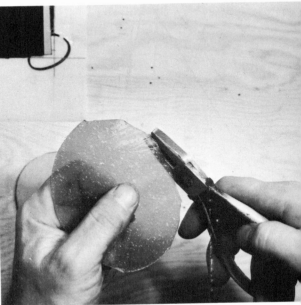

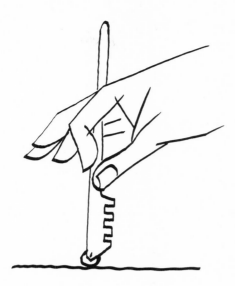

Ready? Press the selected pattern piece firmly to the glass with one hand, spreading your fingers to distribute the pressure evenly. Take the cutter in the other hand. There are variations in the grip. We recommend the position pictured here. It is very important that the cutter be perpendicular to the glass. The cutter should also be comfortable to handle and easy to sight along.

Begin at the point farthest from you and draw the cutter toward you. But don't start at the very edge of the glass; this will cause chipping. Instead, begin and end an eighth of an inch or so from the edges. It is the nature of most glass to continue breaking more or less in the direction of the line. Obviously, pressure on the cutter should be even for the entire length of the cut. With adequate, uniform pressure, you will hear the *scritch* of your cutter from start to finish; and a clearly visible, uninterrupted line will mark the desired contour of your cut.

How much pressure is necessary? The best answer we can give sounds facetious and smug: *enough but not too much.* Lean into it too much and you may break the glass. At best, your cut will be erratic and inaccurate. Go at it too lightly and you will break the glass when you attempt to part it. (No amount of tapping will make up for a weak cut.)

Stance, bench height, the sharpness of your cutter, the differing nature of the material—all will influence the direction and degree of pressure. The few observations we can make that will apply to *most* situations are:

(1) Position yourself so that you are able to reach the cutter and draw it to you without losing your balance or shifting your stance.

(2) Keep your wrist locked; power should be delivered in a direct line from the shoulder whenever possible.

(3) Make sure that your workbench is absolutely wobblefree, and that the glass is flat on its solid surface.

If the score is a bit uneven or if the glass is thick or uneven in texture, you will need to tap. Otherwise, you probably will not. It does no harm, however, and we advise tapping at first, just for practice.

One more pointer at this stage: you can't go over a line more than once without messing it up. Try to get it right the first time.

PARTING THE GLASS

Pick up the glass. Grip it firmly near the edge, on both sides of the line. Apply even pressure away from the line and down. Snap! You are now hold-

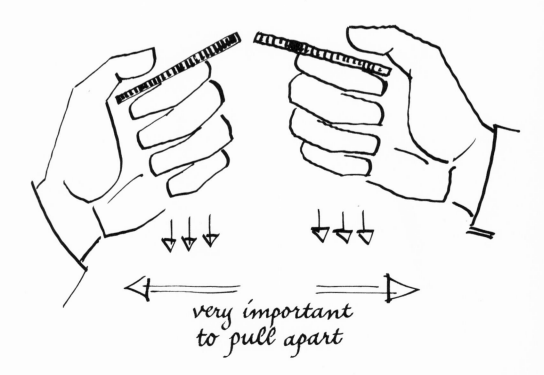

very important to pull apart

ing two pieces of glass. With any luck, one of them is approximately the same size and shape as the pattern piece. Congratulations.

If the sheet from which you are cutting is too big to be picked up and held comfortably by, or very near, the edge, rest one end on the bench. You need leverage to snap the glass, but that doesn't mean that the entire sheet has to be lifted.

Perhaps the glass didn't part where you intended it to. Try again. And again. Use up three or four dollars' worth of window glass in practice. The skill you gain in the process will be invaluable in all future operations. (You may decide to cut the entire pattern in cheap glass. Not a bad idea, if you think you need that much practice.)

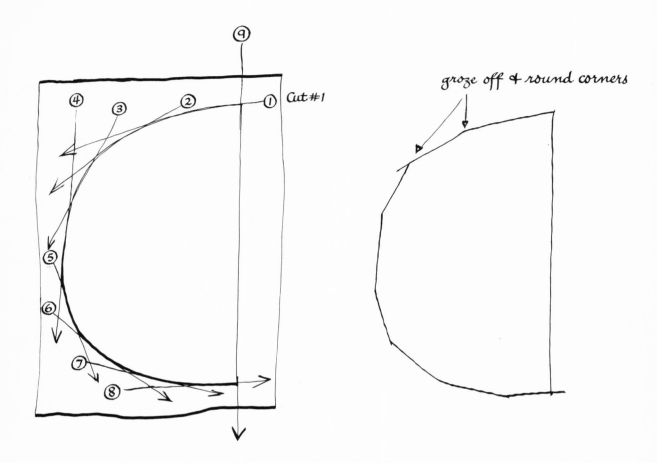

Cut #1

groze off & round corners

Some final hints on cutting. If you can't make one continuous curved cut, make several straight cuts. Then round the corners by grozing (see page 43). Remember, after making each cut, to break off the piece of glass before going on to another cut. See the sketches included here for a couple of additional hints.

We have put you off long enough. Select a piece of stained glass, a matching section from your pattern, and begin. Just keep in mind that the cutting process as described is somewhat idealized. Glass varies not only in color but also in thickness, hardness, and texture, from type to type and from maker to maker. If all glass were as smooth and easy to work as window glass, the cutting would be as simple as slicing cheese. But then the finished work of the stained-glass craftsman would be static and bland.

The rippling, bubbled irregularities that frustrate the craftsman are the very features that bring glory to his work. You selected your materials on the basis of their beauty and suitability; they're perfect for the job. And they *can* be cut. Here's how.

Perhaps you have walked on glazed, crusted snow, falling through with every other step. Bubbles on the surface of the glass provide the same staggering

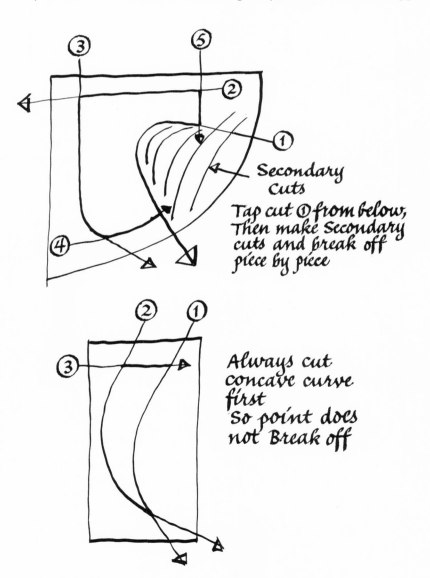

Secondary Cuts

Tap cut ① from below, Then make Secondary cuts and break off piece by piece

Always cut concave curve first
So point does not Break off

course for the cutter. While this cannot be avoided when working with certain types of glass, it needn't doom your plans. When the cutter grinds to a halt in a pocket or bubble, don't attempt to muscle it through. Lift it instead, move it just a fraction, and continue your cut. You may have to repeat this a number of times along your score; but if the cut is firm and otherwise clean, the glass should part true.

Thick glass presents another challenge. Some of it is thicker at and near the edges of a sheet than in the middle. If this is the case, put the glass on one or two sheets of newspaper to compensate for the unevenness. Your cutter will produce the same reassuring surface sound with this glass that it does with thinner material. Now tap along the underside of the cut to create internal fracturing. The glass won't break—at least not where you want it to? Tap harder. There is still plenty of solid substance between the score, the fracture, and the bottom surface. Don't hammer; just be a bit more resolute. The glass should part.

It didn't? Then take up your grozing pliers, pad the glass with folded soft cloth on one side of the score, take a firm grip with the pliers (instead of your hand), and with the additional leverage they provide—twist. Use your free hand on the other side of the score to provide the opposing pressure.

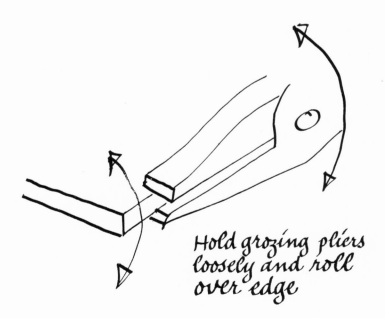

Hold grozing pliers loosely and roll over edge

Sometimes a piece of glass (especially flashed glass) won't score. The surface is extra hard and the cutter skates across it, leaving no impression. In most cases, turning the glass over will solve the problem. The glass is harder on one side than on the other.

You have cut your first piece, following the pattern as closely as you could. Before going on to the next piece, you should trim and dull this one. Hold the pattern piece over the cut glass. They don't have to match perfectly, although they should be close. If the glass is much smaller (by more than between 1/16 and 1/8 inch), you will have to either cut another piece or adjust your entire plan (which is clearly ridiculous). If, however, it is larger in places to roughly the same degree, you can *groze* away the excess.

GROZING

The notches in the cutter head can be used for this operation. Notice that they are of different widths—one for thin glass, the other for thick. With care, you can use the appropriate one to chew away (groze) the excess material. This is not a wrenching operation; a hefty bite and a muscular twist will surely break the glass. Be a bit dainty; nibble.

However, we like grozing pliers for this job rather than the cutter. The leverage is better and the job goes faster, with less chance of breakage. The same general rules apply: don't bite deeply and don't wrench. Use just the tips of the jaws for a lone protrusion; or take a narrow side grip with the jaws for an extended oversize edge. A grozed piece is not clean-looking, but inasmuch as the edges will be lapped with lead it really doesn't matter.

DULLING THE GLASS

Glass is dangerously sharp—another simpleminded observation perhaps, but one often forgotten in the heat of creative activity. A cleanly cut piece has the edge of a scalpel and cannot be handled safely. Gloves offer some protection but are impossibly cumbersome. Take this precaution instead: when you finish cutting each piece, take a scrap of glass and scrape its edge along the fresh-cut edge at right angles. This step takes only seconds and reduces considerably the risks involved in handling the pieces during assembly. (It doesn't guarantee that you won't cut yourself; you will, countless times.)

Keep your bench brush handy, too. Tiny crumbs and chips embed themselves readily in hands and elbows. Once buried, they cause nasty infections.

PREASSEMBLY

At this point, the cartoon becomes a template. Take the pattern pieces and the cut pieces and lay them both on the matching sections of the cartoon, with the glass on top. What you're doing now is preassembling your panel without the lead. If you don't follow this procedure, you are bound to lose pieces, confusing them with accumulated scraps. Also, you will find it simpler and faster to work from a template than from a stack of pieces.

When the cutting is complete and the panel has been laid out on the cartoon, stop long enough to put away the scrap glass. Then get out the glazing knife, hammer, a few nails, lathekin, a couple of lath strips 12 inches long, and a block of wood 2 inches square. (Lath and block dimensions needn't be exact.)

ASSEMBLY

The working drawing should be taped to the workboard or directly to the bench. You will be working on the surface of this drawing, so fasten it securely. Don't use tacks; they'll only get in the way.

Nail one glazing (lath) strip so that it runs from bottom to top of the drawing along the left dimension. Its inside edge should follow exactly the full-size line on the drawing. The other glazing strip gets nailed along the bottom dimension, again abutting the full-size line. To make certain that the strips are square with each other, use a right angle.

You recall that we agreed before making the cartoon that the outside lead would be 3/8 inch. If you don't recall *why* we therefore advised the 3/16-

inch margin between the full-size line and the cut-size line, do go back and review. Otherwise, get out the lead.

Because lead is extremely soft, it has kinked and twisted from handling. It won't be usable until you have straightened it and opened up the flanges. Do that now. Lock one end of the strip in your vise. Grip the other end firmly with pliers and pull. Make sure that you and the vise have a good grip. If either lets go, you'll take a pratfall.

Pull evenly; don't yank. You will know when you have stretched the lead far enough. Keep it taut with one hand now; and with the other, draw the lathekin (or the tip of the cutter handle) along the flanges, opening them evenly.

You need only two pieces of lead for now—one for each leg of the right angle you have formed with the laths. Cut these border leads about an inch longer than finished size. There's a trick to cutting, by the way; you can't go at it as if it were salami. Score the lead lightly with the knife point to mark the course of the intended cut. Then rock the knife gently through the lead. This way you will avoid squashing it. The lead *will* flatten slightly at the cut, but you can easily open the ends with the knife.

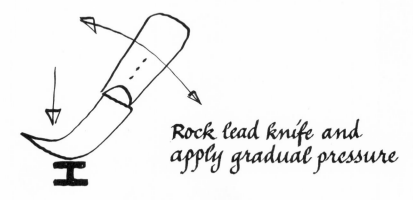

Rock lead knife and apply gradual pressure

This happens if you press too hard.

Pry open ends of flanges

Fit the two border leads inside the angle formed by the lath strips. The bottom left corner, where the two leads meet, is joined very simply. Just slip one piece into the other at right angles. Open up the channel of one sufficiently to accommodate the other.

The construction process should move swiftly from this point, but the way is fraught with pitfalls. Don't jump ahead of our instructions, therefore; and study the pictures closely. (They will better explain the subsequent steps than will the text.)

Stained glass is a combined art-architecture medium which provides most of its own structural support. In limited expanses it needs no bracing beyond that provided by the lead itself. Because the lead is an integral part of the design rather than an externally imposed structural necessity, the marriage of function and form is a good one, from both an artistic and an architectural point of view.

We mention this again because the craftsman must always be aware that his work—at least the kind we describe here—is *functional* art. The design and construction of a panel such as yours should reflect this truism. The finished work, even though you may not actually mount it in a partition, should be *solid* as well as beautiful.

The small panel we have constructed for illustrative purposes could, if properly mounted, withstand a full gale. In fact, it is stronger than a windowpane of similar size. See that yours is, too. While its construction will involve variations from ours, basic techniques are the same. Common sense, combined with illustrations and instructions, will see you through.

Start building from the lower left-hand corner of the design. Insert the first piece of glass into the channels of both border strips. You may have to open the flanges a bit for an easy flush fit, using cutter handle, knife edge, or lathekin. (Be careful with the knife. Lead becomes chewed up and battered very easily.) With the butt of the knife handle, tap the glass into place. But make sure, first, that the knife handle is solid wood at the butt; if the shank of the blade runs clear through the handle, the piece will probably shatter with the first blow. To avoid this, use a block of wood and your hammer instead. Don't be afraid to give the glass a smart tap; just don't hammer it.

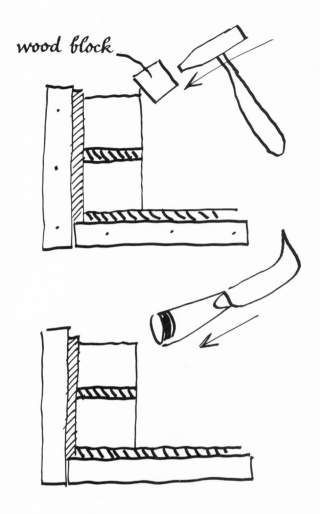

wood block

Now check the fit of the piece against the working drawing beneath it. They should match closely. The insertion of this piece, and virtually all subsequent pieces, prior to applying the lead provides a running check on the *actual* fit of the glass compared with the fit required by the plan. If they are at variance by more than fractions, the overall dimensions of the panel will be off. Even if the finished size of the work is of no real concern, you should follow your original plans. Why be sloppy?

Remove the piece so that it may be fitted with lead. You can leave it in place to perform this operation—indeed, you won't always find it possible to remove it; but measuring and applying the lead is usually easier with the glass in hand.

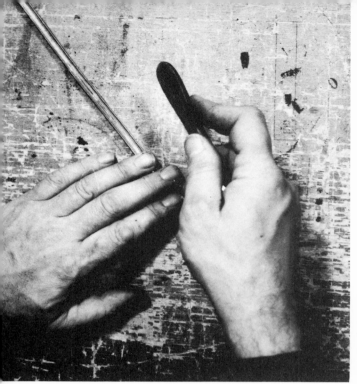

Opening up the channels in the lead. The cutter handle is a useful tool for this operation.

The glazing knife should be kept sharpened. A carbon stone is used here.

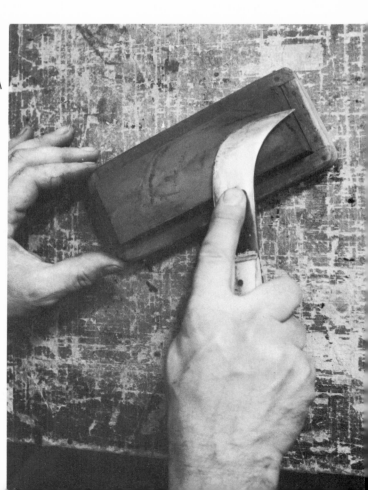

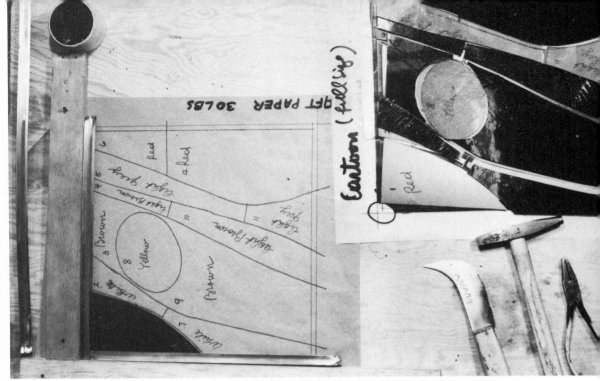

Initial preparations for assembly. Lath strips are tacked in place at the full-size edges of the working drawing. The border lead is laid in place and the first piece of glass is inserted.

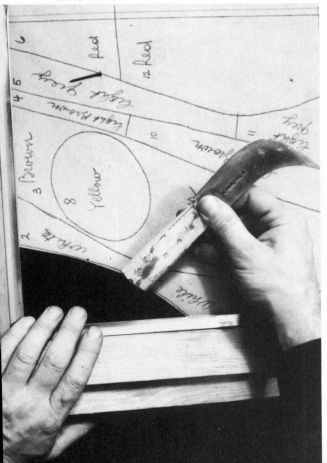

Tapping the first piece firmly into place with the knife handle.

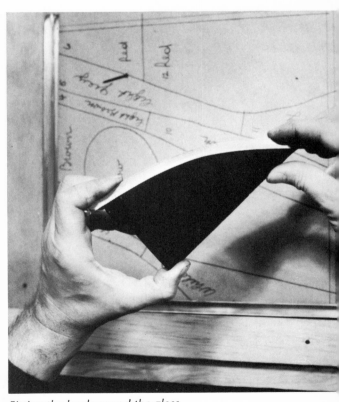

Fitting the lead around the glass.

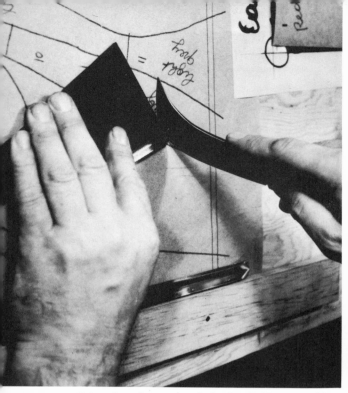

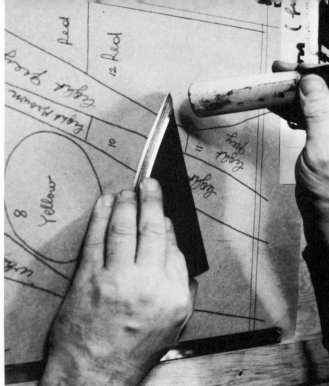

Trimming the ends of the lead. Use a rocking motion with the knife.

Flattening the ends of the lead. Tap very gently.

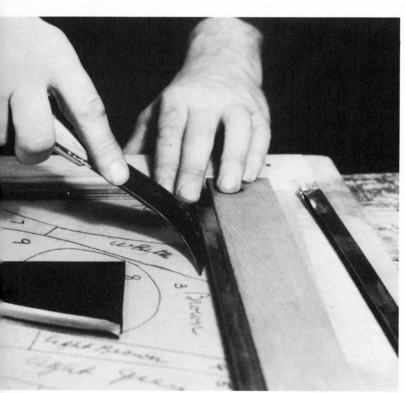

Opening up the channel for reinsertion of the piece.

Flaring the border lead to accommodate the piece.

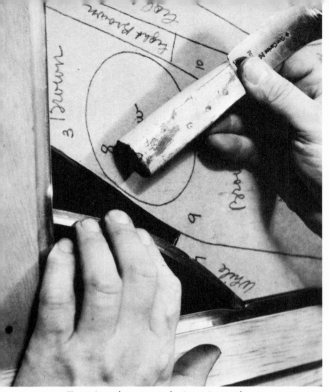

Tapping the second piece into place.

Again, the channel must be opened for a deep, secure fit.

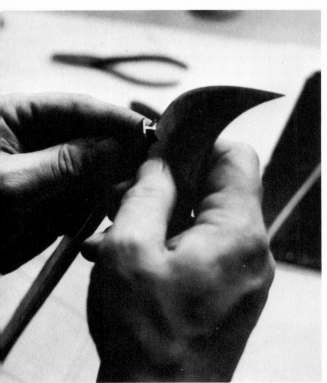

Because the lead is so soft, flanges frequently must be opened up after cutting.

Interlocking two pieces of lead.

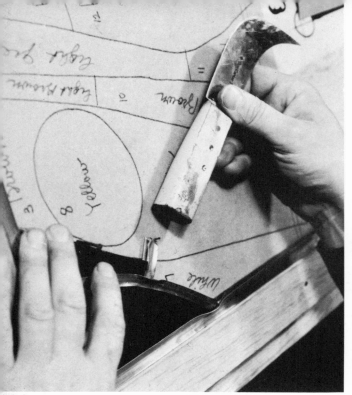

Tapping the lead very gently into place.

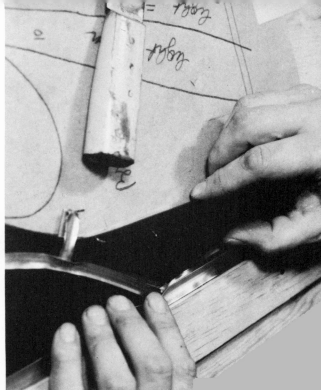

Inserting the third piece.

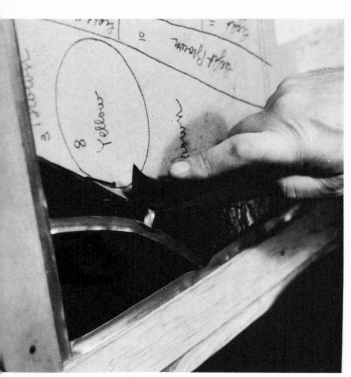

Cutting off the excess lead as closely as possible. Notice the slight undercutting angle of the blade. This will insure that both the top and bottom lead flanges are flush.

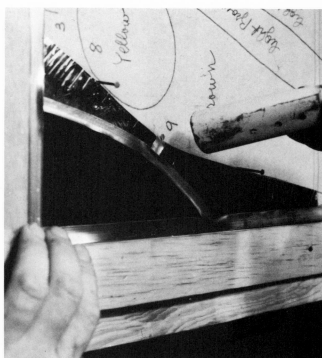

Tapping down the lead to flatten it.

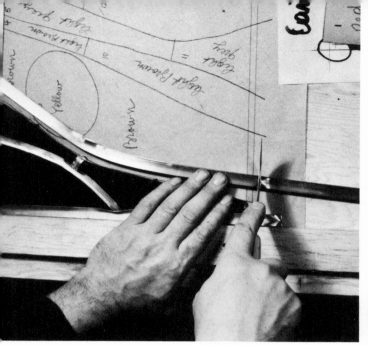

Cutting a long piece of lead prior to fitting. Notice that some excess is left for later trimming.

Pressing the lead around a circular piece and joining it as closely as possible. The ends of the lead should butt against each other.

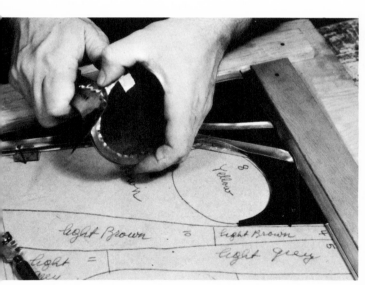

Shaving off excess lead to allow for close fit.

Insertion of the circular piece. Notice that the lead must be flared widely. Notice also the small square of tape which keys the position of the cut circular piece to conform to the working drawing.

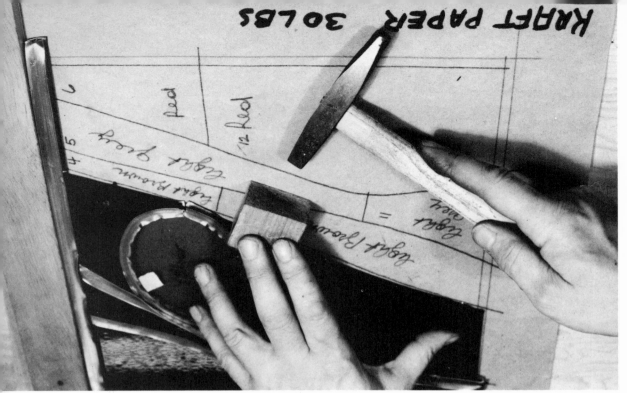

Small block of wood absorbs the shock of the hammer blow. Never strike the glass directly with a hammer.

Assembly is nearly complete.

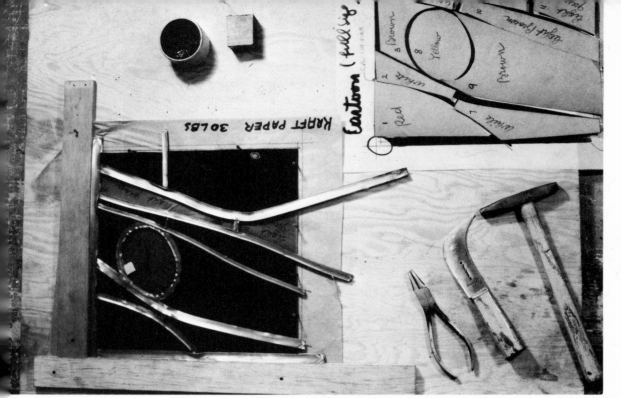

All pieces in place, the work is now ready for trimming and insertion of remaining border lead.

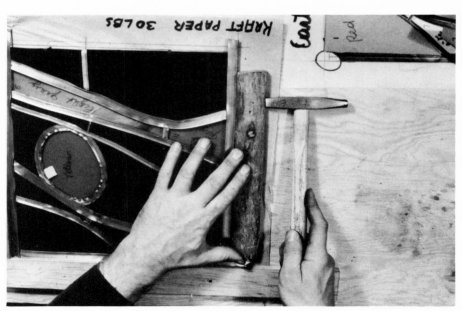

Border lead is tapped into place after final trimming.

Interlocking the border lead at the corners.

Lath strips hold the work together on all four sides.

Lead is now flattened at all joints. The handle of the glazing knife can also be used for this operation.

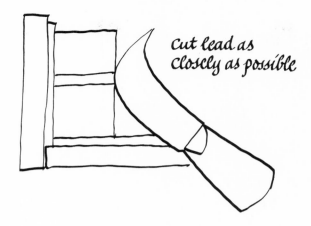

cut lead as closely as possible

Select a piece of lead. Your original sketch and your limited inventory will determine what width of lead to use for this first interior line. You *can* depart from the original plan. Remember that no matter how wide the *interior* leading is, it won't affect the fit.

Stretch the lead. (We won't mention this again. Just remember to stretch and open every piece of lead.) Lay the strip along the edge of the glass, estimate its length, and cut, leaving an ample overhang. Then slip the glass into the channel, working and shaping the lead as you fit it to the glass. Now cut the lead as closely as possible.

Notice that in our first piece the interior lead doesn't interlock at exact right angles with the border leads. Unless your panel is comprised of a series of rectangles, yours probably won't either. Cut the ends of the lead at an angle appropriate to the fit. Always. The angle needn't be exact; an approximation by eye will do. What matters is a snug, neat fit.

The small margin of interior lead that will be inserted into the channels of exterior lead should be flattened slightly. Use the knife handle again. And open slightly the flanges of the exterior lead at the intended joint. Insertion of one into the other should now be easy. Once the lead has been interlocked, tamp the joint lightly to secure it.

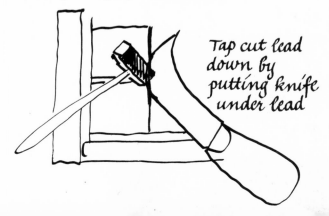

Tap cut lead down by putting knife under lead

The choice of the next piece to be fitted requires a bit of thought. The second piece should support the first, locking it into the border leads and using it as a foundation for its own support. The first piece is a keystone of sorts, at least until the work has been locked together on all sides and soldered. Each subsequent piece should build out from the base, not unlike an inverted pyramid. The difference is that a pyramid is made from uniform pieces in close geometrical relationship to one another—while your panel isn't. Keep the analogy in mind, however; it's the best one we can think of.

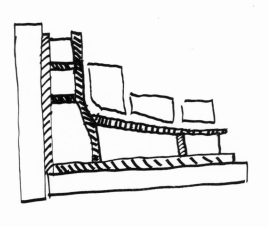

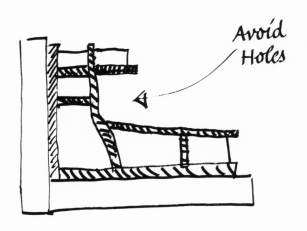

Avoid Holes

The diagram shown here should help, too. Try to detect the logic in the building pattern, and adapt it to fit your own construction. Notice that each piece provides support—and pressure—for the pieces already fitted. If you don't lock things up as you go along but leave gaps to be filled later, the end result will be a wobbly, inexact product. Therefore, determine the exact sequence in advance, and number the steps on your working drawing.

What about the lengths of the leads? Short strips that hold just one piece and conclude? Or long pieces that range uninterrupted across the panel? Again we're forced to generalize, inasmuch as choice of lengths depends largely on your own design. Thus:

(1) Long, uninterrupted lines aren't as interesting as shorter and/or curved lines.
(2) Neither are they as supportive.
(3) It is easier to work with shorter pieces.

There will be fewer awkward bends and kinks in the lead if you avoid running the same strip in and out of tight curves. *Generally speaking,* that is. In most cases, the design will narrow the choice of lengths.

Until the entire panel has been locked up on four sides and soldered, some temporary means of piece-by-piece locking will be necessary. Otherwise, your snugly fitted pieces will loosen the moment you remove finger pressure. Nailing will solve the problem of holding things in place while you turn to other matters. You won't have to nail every piece in the construction. Key pressure points will reveal themselves as you build, and nails will secure them. (Don't puzzle over how the nails will fit into the final creation; they are removed as you go along.)

Drive the nails—two or three will do it—just deeply enough to hold, at the angle diagramed in the sketch. If the outer edge you wish to secure has already been inserted into the lead channeling, use a small block of wood between nail and lead. If you don't, the lead will get dented. When you are ready to fit the next piece, remove the nails.

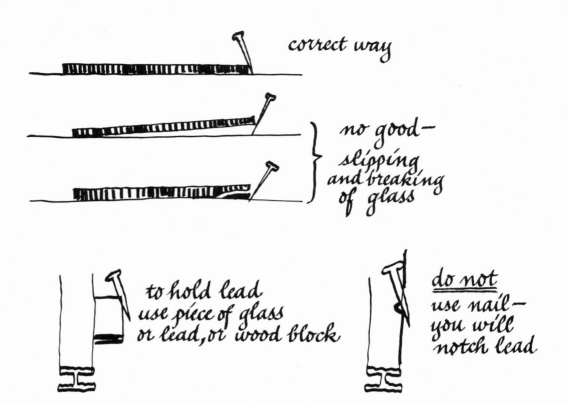

correct way

no good—
slipping
and breaking
of glass

to hold lead
use piece of glass
or lead, or wood block

do not
use nail—
you will
notch lead

When all the pieces have been fitted, trim off the ends of lead that protrude beyond the pattern. For a flush fit, angle the cut in; don't cut square. Then fit the remaining border strips. (Make sure that they are the same width as the first two.) Two more lath strips, tacked firmly into place, will lock the construction all around.

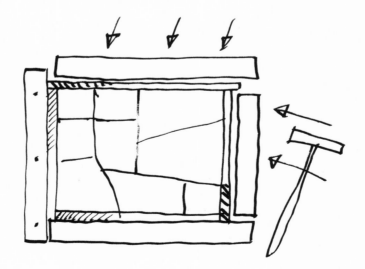

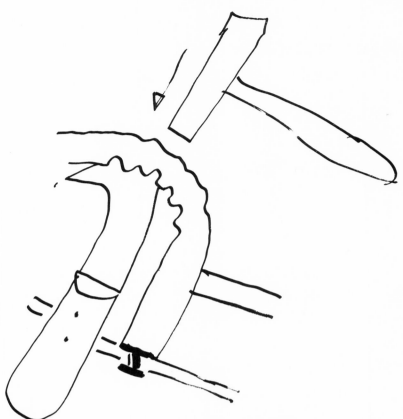

To straighten out kinks,
put cutting knife under lead
and flatten with a hammer

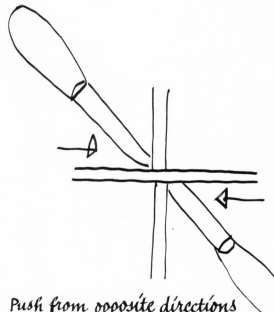

Push from opposite directions
with stopping knife to make
sure leads meet squarely

Make one final check before soldering. Are the leads smooth, flat, without gouges or kinks? Are there any considerable holes between lead and glass? Do the lead joints meet squarely, neatly? This is the last practical opportunity to make corrections. Finally, flatten down all lead joints with a hammer.

SOLDERING

Your soldering iron must be "tinned" to work properly. That is, the tip should be coated with a thin layer of solder for effective heat diffusion. The simplest way to do this is to drop a bit of solder and oleic acid onto a non-flammable surface—a metal ashtray, for instance—and dabble the heated tip of the iron in it until a coating is formed.

You will find that the soldering operation will go swiftly and simply. It requires little practice to make solid, attractive joints; and what few mistakes you do make will be simple to correct. Therefore, preliminaries aren't really necessary. *But caution is.*

Unplug the iron when it won't be in use for the next 15 minutes or so. And don't just put it down anywhere. It should be placed in the same spot every time, preferably at the very edge of the work area, on a cradle or bracket to keep the tip off the bench.

Don't touch the metal shaft below the wooden handle. It is nearly as hot as the tip. And don't plunge the iron into water to cool it or clean it.

So much for safety. Maintenance amounts to keeping the screws tight and cleaning the tip often with a medium-fine file (after which you will have to retin).

With a small brush, apply oleic acid to all joints of the panel. The acid creates a bond between lead and solder and facilitates the smooth flow necessary for good joinery. Now work out from the solder coil four or five inches of free solder. You needn't cut it off; the coil is handier to grip than a random length and will protect your fingers from occasional burns caused by heat creeping up the solder.

Tinning the soldering iron. (The tinning dish is a jar top.)

Oleic acid is applied to the joints—very sparingly.

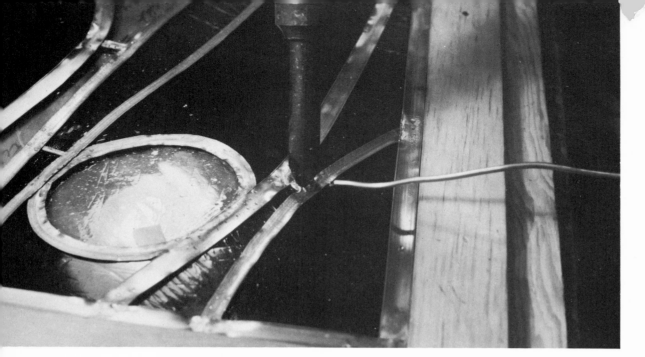

Soldering joints. Make sure every one is soldered.

To make sure that the iron is hot enough, test by melting a piece of solder in the tinning dish. Flow should be smooth and immediate. To make sure that the iron isn't *too* hot, press it against a scrap of lead. If the lead begins to melt under the iron, unplug it. Soldering of this type requires frequent cooling and reheating of the iron. Don't stop soldering; just maintain a reasonably constant temperature by switching the iron on and off.

It takes only a small piece of solder—1/8 inch—to make a joint. Begin the job by laying just the tip of the solder across the junction of the leads. Now press firmly with the iron, flowing the solder in a quick, crisscross motion. The entire operation should have consumed perhaps five seconds and 1/8 to 1/4 inch of solder. Don't use much more than that; joints don't improve in strength or appearance with an excess of solder. The result of this first attempt should be a neat, flat, dull-silver joint roughly in the form of a cross. If so, press on.

If not, what went wrong? If the solder failed to flow and bond smoothly— if the joint is grainy, lumpy, bedecked with globules—either you haven't followed directions or your iron is at fault. Let's explore the former possibility:

(1) You bought the wrong kind of solder.
(2) You forgot to apply the oleic acid.
(3) You didn't heat the iron to the proper temperature.

These factors, singly or combined, will make for weak, sloppy joints.

You are nearly done by now; and if you have come this far, things must be going rather well. So don't rush at this point. Scrutinize the side you have just finished soldering. Redo any weak-looking spots by melting away the original solder and starting fresh. Also, consider *patching* those joints where lead and glass are not firmly met.

If, for instance, you spot a corner where the edge of the glass is just barely covered (or not quite covered) by the lead, whittle a small, flat piece from scrap channeling, fit it snugly into the corner, apply a touch of oleic acid, and solder it into the existing joint. It won't show in the finished work.

At this point, before soldering the second side, you can still change a piece of glass if you are not satisfied with the whole effect. Just pry up the flanges of lead around the piece with your stopping knife or glazing knife, remove the glass, and take your pattern and cut another piece. Then reinsert it and press down the flanges.

Now solder the second side, following the same steps. You will have to remove the lath strips first, but don't bother to refit them; the solder you

Putty is forced between lead and glass, and pushed into place with the thumb.

Flattening the flanges with the lathekin. Excess putty will ooze out, and can then be picked up with a pointed stick.

Whitening is sprinkled on and wiped off. Then the work is scrubbed vigorously with brush.

The finished panel.

have applied will hold the panel together. When you've finished, remove as much of the oleic acid as you can with a rag.

Just another half hour. That is all it will take for puttying and final cleaning. Work the putty in between the lead and the glass with your fingers. Now, with the lathekin, press the lead flanges down. The excess putty that is forced out onto the glass can be picked up with a pointed stick traced around the edges of the lead. (It isn't necessary to putty both sides of the panel unless it is to be exposed to the weather, but do it anyhow.)

Unless you are an impossibly fastidious craftsman, your panel is by now a smeared, gummy mess. To remove the residue of oleic acid, putty, and grime, sprinkle the panel liberally with whitening and scrub it away vigorously with your brush. A couple of applications may be necessary for a sparkling, smudgefree finish. A note of warning here: don't put this job off. Once it has become sticky, the oleic acid is extremely difficult to remove.

The work is complete. *Don't drop it!*

Working with Laminated Glass

Now that you are a qualified glass cutter, you are ready for fussier work. In some respects, glass lamination is more exacting than traditional glass art, mostly because there is no lead to hide ragged edges or an imperfect fit. In this form, antique glass is bonded directly to a clear-glass base with clear epoxy; and the cut pieces must meet cleanly for an acceptable job. Without lead and solder to worry about, the work goes faster. For the same reason, however, you should spend a bit more time and care in choosing shapes and colors. The design is wholly a matter of color, texture, and shape, without the supportive accent and delineation provided by lead.

There need be no practical limit set on the area of glass to be used for lamination, for this technique requires no basic support beyond that of the surface to be laminated. You can do an entire glass wall, therefore, should such an expanse lend itself to this treatment. Because epoxy is terrifically strong and resistant to extremes of temperature, the work need not be confined to stationary, inside situations. Windows and doors of clear glass—even those directly exposed to the weather—often make suitable settings for stained-glass lamination. (The laminated side should face indoors, of course.)

Stained glass is often used to block an unsightly view, or to keep neighbors and passersby from peering in. Such functional installations are fine—but your glasswork should be more important and beautiful than the view you block with it. Don't lose sight of artistry in favor of mere camouflage or increased privacy—even in a bathroom window. Look beyond the temptation to blanket completely a sheet of clear glass with color. In most cases your work will be enhanced by open areas of light incorporated into the design and combined with the outside view.

We warned at the outset that we weren't going to offer a series of projects in stained glass. We won't then, give you a recipe for making a room divider representing the flag, or a laminated bar front for your rumpus room. Use your own imagination in applying the technical advice that follows; the process will work in almost any situation involving flat glass.

TOOLS AND MATERIALS

Plate glass is the most suitable surface for large laminations; for standard windows, regular window glass is all right. The technique won't work well with Thermopane or plexiglass. The best guide to thickness (*gauge*) is your local glass supplier. Tell him the size of the planned piece. (He'll need to know anyhow, for he will cut the overall dimensions.) And follow his advice about thickness. Logically enough, gauge will increase in proportion to overall size. The cost of clear plate glass—1/4-inch gauge—averages 2 dollars per square foot, depending on waste and any special kind of cutting you may order.

In general, and particularly if the finished work is to be mounted in a window or door frame, allow for at least a half-inch margin all around. Otherwise, the molding into which the work is to be fitted will overlap the design area.

For your first efforts, you should have plenty of stained-glass scraps left from your work with the leaded panel, along with a few good-sized pieces. The bonding agent is clear, slow-drying *epoxy*, which can sometimes be bought at a hardware store but may have to be ordered from a supplier. One gallon of epoxy covers from 200 to 500 square feet, depending on the thickness of the bond. At the same time buy some epoxy cleaner.

You will also need a small *spatula* for spreading the epoxy, although a table knife will do; *rubber gloves*; a *vitrified silicone stone* (available at Sears Roebuck); and *grout* (Kwick Solder, available in hardware stores, or any of the cold solders, or epoxy mixed with lampblack).

All the other materials you'll need you have already accumulated. The few basic supplies, almost all available locally, are another factor in making this an attractive medium for the amateur.

Before you begin a work of considerable proportion or detail, experiment; practice a bit. Start out using a small piece of window glass and a tube of epoxy. Let's hope that the colors of your stained-glass scraps are compatible. Again we stress that we don't believe in *pure* practice; what you create should, from the first, be pleasing to you.

The pattern-making process for laminated glasswork is virtually the same as for traditional stained-glass paneling (see pages 25–27). Sketch, cartoon, working drawing, pattern copy—but you don't have to worry about full size versus cut size; just leave the suggested extra half inch beyond the actual design area. (If, for instance, you intend to mount this first small panel in a window frame, measure the entire area to be covered, and subtract 1/4 inch from both dimensions to allow a bit of leeway for fitting. This will give you the correct measurements for the *clear-glass* sheet.) This measurement should be taken from all the edges of the sheet so that the molding which holds the window in place will not touch the actual laminated design area.

Measure the width of the molding and make any necessary adjustments in these general instructions. (And take all measurements at least twice, just to be on the safe side.)

Because there is no lead involved in laminating, it would seem to follow that you needn't allow for spacing between the pieces of stained glass in your design. After all, they are supposed to fit like the pieces of a jigsaw puzzle, with nothing in between. They won't, though—so you might as well make use of the shears or your razor blade device when cutting the pattern. We're often a fraction off in cutting glass; chances are you will be too. The small margin that your shears provide between the pattern pieces is, literally, a margin for error. (Later you can fill in any spaces between the pieces with grout. Don't worry; from three feet away it won't show.)

Have you taped the cartoon to the work surface? Do so; again it will function as the master plan for your assembly. You can also repeat the process of tacking (with adhesive spray or loops of tape) the pattern pieces to the cartoon as you cut them. For a small work with relatively few pieces this isn't really essential, though—unless you run the kind of shop where things tend to get lost. *Do try to make clean cuts.* You really shouldn't count on grozing your way into a good fit, for reasons we have already explained.

Let us repeat that as you cut the glass, dull it. You have already cut yourself enough times to know that our warnings were well advised. This time we aren't thinking only of your benefit. Remember that the edges of the glass do not get buried in lead; they remain exposed. You will be embarrassed, if not horrified, if a guest trails his hand admiringly over your work and walks away bleeding. To save friends and carpeting, use the silicone stone for final dulling and smoothing. Scraping glass against glass is not enough to remove the hazard of exposed edges. Furthermore, the silicone stone treatment will improve the appearance of your work.

To hold the clear glass firmly in place while you are laminating, nail two lath strips onto the work surface to form a right angle at the bottom left corner of the working drawing. (This is the same step as that we followed with the leaded-glass panel.) When you place the glass over the working drawing, the strips will keep it from sliding about.

Mask out any areas that you intend to leave clear of lamination. This is much easier and neater than slathering the entire piece with epoxy and cleaning off the excess later. If you lay the masking tape fairly accurately along the lines delineating the clear areas, you'll have no trouble nipping off with a razor blade the few spots where the edge of the tape protrudes into adjoining segments.

You have probably sensed by now how very simple the actual laminating is. We won't complicate it with an excess of instructions past this point. What follows will work for surfaces of any size on which a single layer of stained glass is to be laminated. And it is as easy as sticking trading stamps in a book.

One warning: it is difficult to the point of near-impossibility to work on vertical surfaces. The epoxy runs; the stained glass can't be held satisfactorily flush against the base glass surface; and air pockets are almost sure to form between the layers of glass. So either plan to do your work in advance of installation, or take the glass out of its setting for lamination. In the case of a door or certain types of windows, this isn't much of a problem. For window walls, partitions, and standard sash windows, however, removal can be a ticklish chore.

Using your spatula, cover with an even, thin layer of epoxy the entire area to be laminated. If you have skipped the small practice piece and tackled a large surface, the best advice we can give is that you follow the epoxy manufacturer's instructions on such matters as mixing and drying time, and maximum surface area to be covered in one application. Once you graduate from dollar tube to bulk, following specifications becomes extremely important.

Start laminating with a corner piece. Because the epoxy is clear, you'll be able to align the piece with the appropriate segment of the working drawing beneath. Press the glass firmly into place, making sure that no bubbles or bare spaces are left between the two pieces of glass. Don't concern yourself now with the excess of epoxy that squeezes out when you press the stained glass into place; it is much easier to remove after it begins to set.

Follow with an adjoining piece. The order in which you **glue the pieces** isn't nearly as important in the laminating process as it was when you worked with lead. Then, you had to apply basic engineering principles to ensure structural soundness. Now, it's simply a matter of the jigsaw principle: the work goes more quickly and logically if you build out from a key piece rather than apply pieces at random.

If you followed our advice and began with a work of modest size, the laminating took about fifteen minutes. If you are impatient by nature, you must fight the urge to pick up your work and hold it to the light. The slow-drying epoxy takes a couple of hours just to get rubbery. (Check the manufacturer's specification sheet.) It won't dry hard enough to be moved for 24 hours. All you can do now is a bit of careful cleaning.

When the epoxy does begin to dry enough to take on a rubbery consistency, scrape it away with a razor blade, peel off the masking tape, and do a thorough cleaning job with the epoxy cleaner.

Has it occurred to you that, now that you know the basic technique, you needn't stop with one layer? That you can laminate both sides? That you can build to random thicknesses? That you can laminate the stained glass on edge instead of laying it flat? Or that you can make free-form sculpture without a base sheet?

Probably such ideas have come to mind. If you weren't creative, you wouldn't have read this far. Any of these variations can result in beautiful stained glasswork. We'll sketch out quickly what little additional information you will need and leave the rest to you.

MULTIPLE LAYERS

To build more than one layer of stained glass on the base piece, you should arrange a simple framework. The illustration should make the construction details clear enough; and you can also see that without such a framework the outside edges of the additional laminated pieces may slide out of place before they are set. Heavy cardboard, coated on the inside with paste wax, is strong enough. If you have left a margin for installation purposes, move the framework in so that it will be flush against the outside edges of the additional laminations of stained glass.

You won't want to add an entire layer. It would only serve to cover up the first one. Additional laminations should add accent, color, depth; they shouldn't blot out what lies beneath. So apply the pieces with care, and don't lose sight of the overall impression you're after. Naturally, if you choose to add just a few pieces, perhaps only one or two, you won't need a framework.

SLAB-GLASS LAMINATION

Slab glass is too heavy for the standard laminating technique we have outlined. But that doesn't mean that you cannot incorporate odd pieces of dalle with antique. Of all the processes we go into, this is the only one where we recommend mixing antique and slab glass. A random piece of dalle can highlight an antique-glass lamination and add a jewellike third dimension to the construction.

Whether the slab is incorporated into the basic lamination or as part of an additional element, it should be beveled down so that it is roughly the same thickness at the edges as the antique. (This operation is covered on page 93.) It requires special tools and a bit of practice to facet and bevel slab glass, but the laminating job is simple.

LAMINATED GLASS ON EDGE

Not nearly as tricky as it sounds. What's more, it can yield incredibly striking effects. You can combine this technique with the flat laminating process or build an entire piece on edge. Be aware, in either case, of a couple of obvious limitations. For one thing, you can't let this kind of lamination stand up too high from the clear-glass base. Vary the heights of the pieces, as well as their ridgelines, but don't plan on a construction more than 2 inches tall. This process doesn't lend itself to moving surfaces either, so forget about door and sash window installations. It is perfectly suited for fixed partitions, though, such as nonmoving windows, room dividers, or glass walls.

Fashion a framework for the work. Unless you plan to sandwich just a few vertical pieces and can use C-clamps to span their combined thickness, you will need firm support at both ends of the work to hold the pieces together until the epoxy takes. Make sure to wax the inner surfaces of the framework, or they'll bond to the job. If you *can* span the vertical pieces with C-clamps, use waxed wooden strips between their jaws and the glass. Otherwise, the glass will break.

Cutaway view of several thicknesses of laminated glass

grout

antique glass

cardboard

tape

epoxy

base (clear glass)

laminated glass on edge

Working with Slab Glass

The technique we'll outline in this section is distinctly different from the work you have performed thus far. Slab (or dalle) glass isn't at all the same kind of animal as the fragile stuff you have been using. It is about *seven* times as thick, for one thing. Furthermore, while the traditional stained-glass window is often a wonder of delicacy, a slab-glass construction is more often formidable and massive in appearance. And while the former is definitely windowlike, the latter tends, regardless of function, to look more like a wall. Finally, while one substance most often is suspended in a web of lead, the other is captured in a sturdy mounting of epoxy resin or concrete.

Slab glass resembles more closely man's early efforts at glassmaking than does the thin, transparent substance we have discussed in previous sections. Early glass was thick, dense, difficult to cut—and nearly worthless for transmitting light. It was celebrated, at least in pre-Christian times, not for its practical properties but for its jewellike brilliance. Thus, the Egyptians, probably the first glassmakers, used glass mostly in mosaic settings, not windows. The product was not vastly different from "natural glass"—the substance created by volcanic heat.

The comparison of modern slab glass with that turned out by the craftsmen of ancient Egypt may be more fanciful than real; glassmaking is, as we have explained, a complex art, and we imagine that today's glassmakers would argue with some heat (and justice) that their product is not to be equated with the nearly opaque, lumpy substance of early mosaics. The thread of continuity that connects the glowing dalles in our workshop with the rough beginning efforts of the ancients is, however, too romantic to ignore.

But you are more interested in how to work slab glass—and, truthfully, so are we. If you live near a city of 100,000 or more, you will find examples of slab glass somewhere. Banks, schools, office buildings, civic structures, churches, restaurants—slab-glass art is eminently adaptable to a variety of architectural purposes, much more so than traditional stained glass.

We're assuming your relative lack of familiarity with the medium, which may not be the case with all readers. It is highly unlikely, though, that the typical beginning craftsman knows as much about slab glass as he does about traditional glass. The more examples you study, the more able you will be to judge the nature of the art and to determine how you can successfully translate it into works of your own. Like most artistic mediums, this one requires not only the ability to manipulate materials but also a strong sense of possibilities and limitations.

TOOLS AND MATERIALS

Slab glass is a highly gratifying medium. While it is possible to make aesthetic mistakes, the chances are fewer than with traditional glasswork.

Furthermore, you can see how the construction will look almost from the start; and because the work goes swiftly, you won't have to wait long for a finished product. Nor does this medium require highly refined skills to produce beautiful results.

The only formidable challenge to the worker in slab glass is the cutting. A dalle is 7/8 inch thick, while antique averages 1/8 inch or less. Obviously, they don't cut the same way. As you know by now, traditional stained glass can be shaped to fairly precise and intricate dimensions; but not so slab glass. The best that you can achieve with slab is crude, simplistic shaping. Any departure from a straight-line cut requires chipping with a special hammer, leaving edges that look gnawed and raw. This has important implications for design, which we'll touch upon later. For now, the issue is less aesthetic than practical: how is the cutting done?

The basic cutting instrument is a homemade *anvil*. Its construction will require a bit of scavenging on your part. One essential component is a hardwood log or beam at least 8 inches across and about 18 inches long. A sawmill is the only source of supply we can think of, although a lumberyard

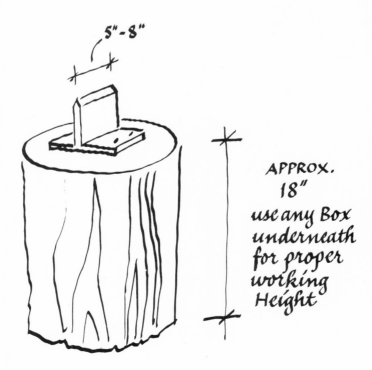

5" - 8"

APPROX.
18"
use any Box
underneath
for proper
working
Height

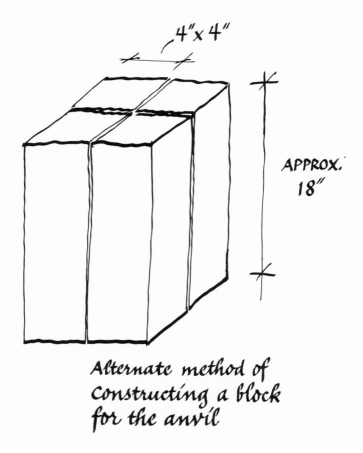

4" x 4"

APPROX. 18"

Alternate method of
Constructing a block
for the anvil

might have something suitable. Your next acquisition should be a piece of steel T-angle—the kind used in heavy construction. As you can see in the accompanying illustrations, you will need only a small piece. The "T" leg of the piece should be at least 3 inches high, and in length 5 to 8 inches. We can almost guarantee that sharp looking in likely places will turn up such a scrap piece. Check construction sites, of course; and also scrap metal dealers, junkyards, blacksmiths, wrecking firms, industrial building supply houses, welding shops—any place where construction steel is in evidence.

Unless you are extremely lucky, the piece you find won't be the right length. That is not a problem, unless it is too large to carry away; for any welding shop can cut it for you. This leaves two more steps in the making of the anvil itself—drilling for the mounting screws and grinding to an edge. A blacksmith should be able to perform both operations. (Blacksmiths, by the way, didn't go out with the horse and buggy; there are lots of them around today.) From your hardware dealer get a half dozen 4-inch wood screws and wide washers, and have three evenly spaced holes drilled or cut through each tang of the "T" to accommodate the screws. The edge should be ground to the sharpness of a dull ax—just barely keen enough to make a clean, even impression. Too sharp a blade will dull quickly against the glass and will also wear unevenly. Furthermore, such an edge presents an unnecessary hazard.

Drill three holes in the log to receive the wood screws. Then mount your "T" anvil squarely and firmly, first making sure that the top and bottom surfaces of the log are flat and even. One last basic step now remains: the log-anvil assembly should be elevated on a platform or box to get it up to optimum working height (about 30 inches).

You have constructed the most important tool you will need for working in slab glass. And while it may have taken some hunting and hard work, the entire job probably hasn't cost much more than 10 dollars. Furthermore, it will serve as well as the ones found in professional shops. Most stained-glass craftsmen make their own anvils exactly the way you made yours.

You will also need a *hammer*. You can obtain a special one designed expressly for working with slab glass, or a mosaic hammer, but you can get by quite nicely with a mason's hammer, which is both cheaper and easier to come by. Masons use them for chipping dried cement from masonry and for cutting and shaping bricks; the working edge is about an inch wide and fairly sharp. While you can make straight cuts through larger pieces of dalle with the anvil alone, you will need the hammer for smaller, trickier work. This same tool also comes into play when the edges or surfaces of the piece are to be faceted. So count the hammer in as basic, essential equipment. Any contractors' supply house will have them in stock for six to eight dollars.

Because the chips fly freely and dangerously, we strongly advise the acquisition of *safety goggles* (about a dollar at your hardware dealer). And pick up a pair or two of *rubber gloves* while you are there—not the kind that keep hands lovely, but the tougher, heavy-duty type. Some people are sensitive to the chemicals in the epoxy hardener with which you will be working. The gloves are sure protection against possible rashes that develop from contact with the bonding agent. You also will need a *glass cutter,* for scratching pattern lines on the surface of the dalles, and a *rubber spatula.* For mixing batches of the epoxy resin neatly and economically, buy a couple of *cardboard* or *plastic buckets,* gallon size; and for measuring out the hardener, a dozen *paper cups* for hot liquids.

Next stop is the lumberyard. If you don't already have a plywood work-board, buy a piece of 3/4-inch at least 20 x 30 inches (about four dollars). And some strips of wood approximately an inch and a quarter wide. Twelve feet of stripping will do.

Slab glass is expensive by comparison with antique glass. Normally, it sells by the pound; it weighs around seven pounds per dalle. We strongly urge you to buy "remnants"—broken pieces of dalle which usually average at least 4 x 6 inches and sell, with no color choice, for about 50 cents a pound, plus shipping charges. For 25 dollars or so you can buy a considerable inventory —easily enough for a half dozen panels of modest size. (Keep in mind that the glass itself takes up only part of the total area; the rest is epoxy or concrete.) Sources of supply are listed in the appendix. Plan on two weeks or more between ordering and delivery.

Epoxy resin is sold in gallon units by most manufacturers. The hardening agent comes in a separate, much smaller can and is always included with the purchase of the epoxy. A gallon of top-grade epoxy costs about nine dollars and is ample for the beginning; we'll show you how to get the most out of it, with a minimum of waste. Suppliers are numerous; your local paint or hardware store will get it for you, but we have also listed sources in the appendix.

Concrete is actually less expensive than epoxy and more readily available. Offsetting factors, however, are that it isn't as easy to work with or as resilient as epoxy. Particularly for installations where the weather side of a construction experiences temperature extremes, epoxy is the better bet; concrete, when uniformly warmed on the inside and sometimes chilled on the outside, often cracks. However, it is otherwise eminently suited to the medium, and you should feel free to try it. Premixed concrete is the simplest to work with. All masonry supply houses and most hardware stores stock it. A 25-pound bag costs about a dollar.

Neither epoxy nor concrete hardens to a particularly attractive finish—at least not an artistically pleasing one. Therefore, most craftsmen coat these areas of their works with *coarse sand* or *marble chips*. These are applied to the surface before the epoxy or concrete dries. *Fine sand* is a necessary ingredient in *all* slab glass–epoxy constructions, not for surfacing but for the molding process. You won't need much of either grade for your beginning projects. All building supply houses have sand, often in small bags. Be sure that the sand you buy is washed and screened of impurities. Building supply houses, florists, and garden shops all carry marble chips, should you decide to use them rather than sand for surfacing. You will want the smallest chips available, fine enough to spread almost as smoothly as coarse sand.

The two basic premises on which this book rests are (a) that you should become sufficiently grounded in the techniques of stained-glass crafting to allow you to depart from them with confidence; and (b) that the training should be enjoyable and rewarding. To ensure that these conditions are met here, we again urge that you begin with a practice piece of modest, uniform dimensions. If you have already decided that your first work in this medium must have a specific, predetermined function, fine. No reason why you shouldn't produce a small window, wall hanging, tabletop, or whatever, on your first try. But don't forget that you are a stranger to the medium; until you have developed some insights into the nature of slab-glass construction, better not to push too far too fast. Virtually all the instructions that follow are easily adaptable to dimensions other than those prescribed.

We observed earlier that this medium is particularly gratifying. To make it doubly so this first time, we'll skip the cutting process entirely and concentrate on actual construction. This is cheating in a sense; nearly all good works, no matter how wildly abstract and random they may appear to be, are the result of painstaking cutting and arranging. Much of the allure of slab glass, however, lies in its *basic* beauty; unlike oil paint in a tube—or even antique glass in a sheet—an odd chunk of dalle is singularly beautiful raw material. Regardless of their accidental shapes, a dozen pieces can be put together in a variety of lovely designs.

Don't mistake this first piece for child's play. Although you can produce a finished panel in less than 4 man-hours, a couple of steps are critical and need close control. Furthermore, this isn't just mindless practice; if you are any kind of artist, you will try your best to make this work distinctly your own creation.

Step One: Clear your workbench. Then cut a sheet of 30-pound kraft paper approximately two feet square and tape it to the center of your workboard. Rule off a square 18 x 18 inches. And be fussy about these measurements—make sure the square *is* square. (It doesn't have to be 18 inches, nor does it have to be a square; these are merely recommended dimensions. If you have determined to depart from them, do at least stick to a rectangle.)

Step Two: Cut the wooden strips to form a frame for the ruled-off area. The frame should be snug and solid, conforming to the outside dimensions of the square. After nailing the pieces together at the corners and fitting the frame over the paper, attach it firmly to the board itself. Finishing nails serve best for this job. Drive them just deep enough to hold, but not too deep for easy removal. The paper stays in place, forming the middle of the frame-paper-workboard sandwich.

Now cut strips of construction paper, heavy kraft, or shirt cardboard to the height of the frame (1-1/4 inches), and long enough to be taped all around the inside face of the frame. Join the ends of the strips by overlapping, not butting, them. This frame lining stops the frame from leaking.

Step Three: Make a paper cone (actually a funnel). A piece of heavy kraft about 12 x 15 inches will do. Fasten the seams inside and out with masking tape. The hole at the narrow end should be small enough to retard the free flow of fine sand to a degree that it may be guided neatly between the pieces of dalle in your design.

Step Four: Lay random pieces of dalle within the framework. Experiment until you hit a pleasing combination of shapes and colors. Some subjective advice about composition:

(1) Uniformity is a bore; by using similar shapes in geometric regularity you run the risk of creating a static work.

(2) Too many small pieces, unless they're very cleverly arranged, produce a cluttered business that has no place in this medium. Don't destroy the bulky power of slab glass by being dainty. Mix large and small, curve and rectangle.

(3) Let the epoxy resin play a large part in your design; its possibilities are infinite. Vary its width; channel its mass artistically among the glass pieces; make it as expressive a part of the pattern as the glass itself.

Aside from overall size, only one design limitation should be noted here: keep the outside edges of the glass at least 1 inch in from the actual borders of the work. The glass should not form any part of the outside edges of the finished piece.

Step Five: Funnel the fine-grade sand around the dalles until they are half buried. Smooth out any slight high or low points with a scrap of cardboard or a brush. The sand should come fully and evenly to the borders formed by the frame.

Step Six: Mix the epoxy resin. A quarter gallon (1 quart) will be ample for the panel we have described. To avoid waste, both now and in future constructions, mark off the gallon can of epoxy into quarters with a felt-tip pen. Do the same with the can of hardener. Now pour a quarter of the epoxy into a bucket and mark the level on the bucket. Pour a quarter of the hardener into a paper cup and, again, mark the level. You now have measures you can use again and again. Mixing the two commits you to action; be prepared to move briskly once the hardener hits the epoxy. The instructions on the can will list approximate drying time under normal conditions; generally the mix won't begin to set for at least 10 minutes.

We urge you to don rubber gloves at this point. The chemicals with which you are working may have no harmful effect on your skin, but until you find out, don't take chances. Stir the mix vigorously with a length of dowel or a spatula until it is uniformly viscous (more or less honeylike), and follow any incidental directions the manufacturer has supplied. With the same funnel you used for the sand, flow the mix evenly around the dalles to a depth just 1/8 inch below the tops of the pieces. The flow can be controlled by squeezing the bottom of the funnel. The mix should run to the very edges of the frame. It should also have flowed into every irregular niche around the dalles. But it won't, so be on the lookout for small hollows and gaps. Fill them by smoothing the mix with a small edge of cardboard.

Step Seven: Sprinkle coarse-grade sand on top. The epoxy matrix will absorb some of it, which doesn't matter. Just keep sprinkling until the entire work is amply covered and the absorption stops. Do it evenly. Don't just dump the sand on.

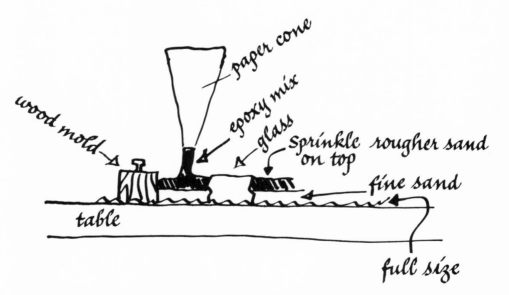

This is all you can do for now. The most frustrating aspect of many artistic endeavors is waiting for the glue to dry. Slab glasswork is no exception.

Step Eight: Next day (or as soon as the epoxy has dried completely), sweep the work clean of excess sand. Whatever sweeps away is excess. The rest is bonded to the epoxy; it would take chiseling to remove it. The first whisks of your bench brush will reveal the sparkling surface of the glass. Seconds later the entire design will emerge. This is a rewarding moment, no matter how often experienced.

Step Nine: Remove the nails that hold the frame to the board. Turn the work over and sweep away the fine sand from both the undersurface of the piece and the work area. This sand served the important function of keeping the epoxy from seeping all the way through to the underside, and thereby enabled you to control the flow of the matrix. Without the sand barrier, the bottom surface would be messy, gapped, and uneven. Also, if the epoxy had been allowed to flow all the way through and around the bottom side, there would be no space left to coat this second side with coarse sand. The epoxy would be flush with the surface of the glass. If you performed the fifth step as directed, you will find that much of the glass remains exposed on the second side, and that the epoxy on this side is coated with a light layer of fine-grade sand. Wet epoxy forms a poor bond with dry epoxy; the sand layer thus provides a necessary gripping surface for the second, final application of epoxy.

Step Ten: Mix another batch of epoxy. The second side will require slightly less epoxy than did the first, although you may find it easier at this point to mix another quarter gallon and throw away what's left. (As you become more proficient—and more cost-conscious—you will find it wise to have another panel set up and ready for pouring. That way nothing is wasted; the excess epoxy is poured directly into the next frame.) After mixing, follow the instructions for pouring, and for sprinkling the coarse-grade sand, as detailed in steps six and seven.

Now let's go on to more complex matters. With your first panel you skipped not just one step, the cutting, but two: you didn't make a pattern. Because your design was pretty much dictated by available scrap glass, you didn't have to. This time, the design is up to you—at least within the limits of your skills and materials. You know what you are about now, much more than before; and your pattern should reflect as much.

Step One: For a specific design, proceed the same way you did with leaded glass—sketches, cartoon to scale, pattern, working drawing (see pages 25–27). Exceptions to the steps outlined previously are as follows:

(1) You don't need special shears or parallel razor blades to cut up the pattern. Use a matte knife, single-edge razor blade, or regular scissors.

(2) You should allow for random widths of epoxy surface, but none narrower than 1/4 inch.

(3) As we cautioned earlier, don't run the glass to the edge of the pattern. This last point needs some qualifying. Notice in the photos (page 95) that the working drawing's outside margins are more than an inch from the frame, and that some of the pieces of glass in the drawing do touch these margins. The area inside the margins is the actual design area (the cut size), the distance between these margins and the frame itself (the full size) is to provide for a bulwark of epoxy.

Step Two: Earlier we advised you to practice cutting with window glass before tackling antique. We wish that such a cheap substitute were available for your initial attempts with slab glass. But no such luck; you have to start with the real thing. In some respects the process is easy. The inherent limits imposed on accuracy and precision by the nature of the substance make even first efforts at cutting acceptable. Most designs are abstract and rough-hewn. Being off a bit, therefore, doesn't matter much. (This may be heretical, but it is honest.) Still, splitting a piece of glass almost an inch thick (and worth four or five dollars) is no light matter.

The anvil should be set up in an out-of-the-way corner of your shop. Place a trash barrel directly behind it to catch the chips. If you shape a curved cardboard backstop and attach it to extend the back rim of the barrel another foot or so, you'll catch twice as many.

Before a piece is shaped to irregular dimensions, it must first be cut to rectangular shape. A standard dalle is 8 x 12 inches—much too large to be mounted. In fact, because of the coefficient of expansion, it isn't wise to use a piece any larger than 6 x 6 inches. So your first cutting job amounts to

reducing in size at least some of those remnants to smaller, regular proportions in order to perform the next step—cutting them to specific shapes.

Straight-line cuts are not difficult. Because remnants average 4 x 6 inches, much of your work has been done for you. The smallest size you can cut to by the method we're describing is 2 x 3 inches, which means you have only two straight cuts to make—the first down the center; then again down the center. To reduce a full-size dalle to sections of 2 x 3 inches would require 15 cuts—not that you would necessarily want 16 pieces of this size. Using bigger pieces is perfectly okay, as we established earlier. But using them just to avoid cutting is cheating. (The panel in the photos uses only one piece larger than 2 x 3 inches.)

Measure off the center line of your first piece; mark it with a grease pencil in a couple of spots; and, using a straightedge as your cutting guide, score the line cleanly with your cutter. Next, align the score over the cutting edge of the anvil. Grip the piece firmly at either edge with the scored surface up, raise it about four inches, and bring it down sharply on the mark. How hard? That's a tough one. The thickness and heft of the glass should communicate to you, in ways we can't, how much pressure to put into the blow. Certainly you shouldn't bring down the piece with smashing force—but if on the other hand you give it a fainthearted tap, you will only chip and mar it. It is most important to perform the operation cleanly and with resolve. A firm, crisp blow will do it.

Scoring a dalle lengthwise.

With a firm blow, the dalle is snapped in two.

Scoring again to further reduce the size of the pieces.

Further reducing the pieces in size. For cuts smaller than this, other means must be used.

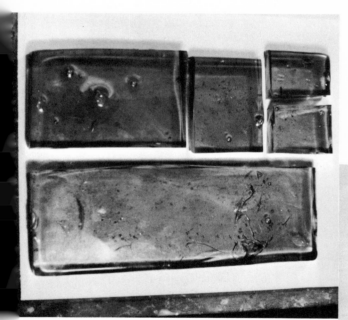

Two alternative ways of segmenting dalles.

Step Three: The next phase of the cutting is to shape the pieces. The pattern should be scribed on each section of glass. Hold the pattern piece in place and mark its outline on the glass with the grease pencil or glass cutter. Then select a piece for cutting to shape. Place the piece on the anvil, gripping it firmly with one hand. The line of the intended cut should be placed directly on the blade edge. Taking your hammer, elevate it two or three inches above the glass. The downswing is slightly arclike, with the weight of the hammer providing most of the force. Another way to put it is that the hammer should not meet the edge of the anvil blade squarely but should instead follow through in a very slight curve toward you. If the hammer edge hits squarely against the anvil edge with the·glass directly

Note the correct angle and direction of the hammer swing in relation to the cutting blade.

To make small cuts, the glass is laid directly upon the anvil and struck firmly with a hammer. Angle of the blow is most important.

between, it becomes a matter of an irresistible force meeting an immovable object. The glass will shatter. Take a close look at the photos of this operation; you will see clearly what we mean. (Although the anvil blade is somewhat different in shape from the one we have described, the principle remains the same.)

For smaller, irregular cuts, the anvil won't serve as well as the block on which it is mounted. Hold the glass against the top of the block, as shown in the photo and sketch, and tap smartly with the hammer. Although truly precise work is impossible, you will be able to fashion fairly clean curves with a little practice.

To shape a small piece for an irregular angle or curve, the glass is rested against the cutting block itself and tapped with the hammer.

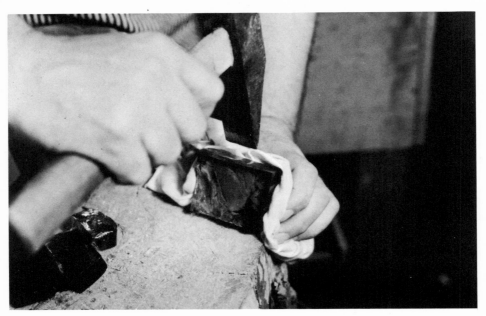

Using the hammer to facet a piece. Note that the piece is held firmly to the block.

Every cut should begin and end rock-solid. This axiom applies to the stability of the anvil, your grip on the glass, and the fall and follow-through of the hammer.

Perhaps you have noticed in your study of other works in slab glass that some of the mounted pieces have a chipped, irregular surface. This is not a special kind of glass but is the result of *faceting,* a simple and most imprecise cutting process. In our opinion, faceted pieces should serve as highlights but should never dominate a work. Used sparingly and with concern for overall effect, their coruscating brilliance is an aesthetic asset. Used excessively, their effect is lost and the results are vulgar.

To facet glass, hold the piece in your hand against the block, cushioning it with layers of flannel. Direct the hammer in a short, arcing swing at the edge of the glass, not the surface. The point of contact should be just below the surface edge. A well-executed cut will leave a shallow, somewhat dished facet. Don't try to cut too deeply. And don't facet the entire piece. Furthermore, don't attempt this technique with very small pieces.

After the frame is nailed in place, the inside is lined with strips of cardboard and taped firmly, to prevent seepage of sand and epoxy resin. The corners, particularly, must be carefully sealed. This is where leaks are most likely to occur.

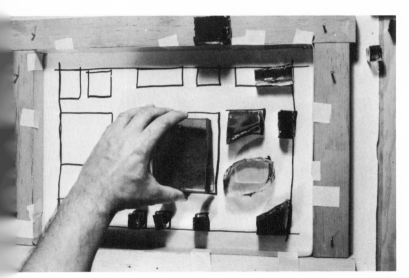

Laying the cut dalles in place.

Fine-grade sand is now poured to a level halfway up the thickness of the dalles, and the sand leveled with a brush.

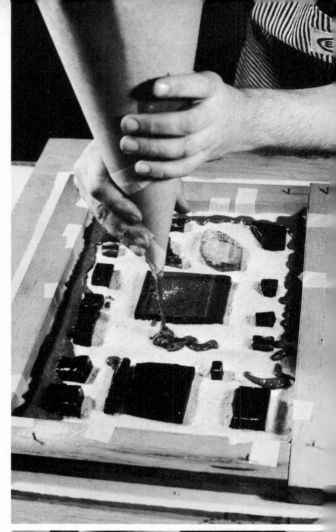

To keep both hands free for pouring the epoxy resin into the cone, place the narrow end of the cone into a can of sand.

Pouring the epoxy resin.

Using a small piece of cardboard to close up gaps and holes.

A final coating of coarse-grade sand
is now sprinkled over the surface.

After the epoxy resin has hardened completely,
the panel is lifted and turned over. This
side is now ready for the epoxy resin and coarse sand.

All the remaining steps—framing, pouring sand and epoxy, smoothing, turning, and so forth—have already been described. We have only one thing to add. If you have included faceted pieces, fill in the gouges below surface level with putty before pouring the epoxy. Otherwise, it will flow into these depressions and cover them. When the work is dry, remove the putty.

Slab glass can be put rewardingly to other, less formalized uses. Full-size dalles, for instance, can be glued directly together in a variety of functional or purely artistic ways. You can form countless geometric shapes for wall hangings, freestanding sculpture, lamp and table bases and tops, simple cubes—whatever strikes your fancy and is structurally feasible. Small pieces and chips can be glued to walls, boxes, bottles, picture frames; mixed with mosaicwork; turned into jewelry; or put to uses we haven't dreamed of. In this medium you need never decry the lack of possibilities.

The finished panel.

Working with Copper Foil

When we promised early in the book to show you how to make a Tiffany-type lampshade, we meant that we would explain the technique Tiffany used. This section won't, therefore, attempt to guide you along lines that will lead to a work consciously imitative of an original Tiffany; but once you have mastered the few simple skills necessary for lampshade construction, you are free to turn them to any style you like. However, Tiffany made much of his own glass—the curved, iridescent, opalescent substance that marks his more striking works. You won't find its type readily in supply houses, despite the recent Tiffany craze.

Copper foil work is the easiest and possibly the most alluring of stained-glass techniques. It is the least traditional and time-honored, and also the most frivolous. Like all artistic mediums, it has finite limits, but decidedly fewer than other kinds of glasswork. So, while we urge you to hold to preconceived patterns in lampshade construction, this restraint needn't apply to related expressions in jewelry, sculpture, or free-form experimentation, which are also in the realm of copper foil technique.

Although this section is focused on lampshade construction, with the technique you will learn here you can fashion nearly anything that touches your imagination. Copper foil is a wonderfully flexible material; it is fast, neat, and inexpensive to work with, and provides an ideal way to involve you and your family in countless stained-glass projects.

TOOLS AND MATERIALS

You already know, and have practiced, all the necessary techniques that apply to copper foil work—patternmaking, glass cutting, and soldering. Furthermore, you have most of the required tools and materials on hand—a soldering iron, cutter, shears, marking pens, workboard; and solder, glass, kraft paper, etc. What special items you'll need for lampshade and jewelry work will be few, easy to find, and inexpensive.

You will probably have to send for the copper foil, although some larger hobby shops may stock it. Copper foil is available to the amateur in two forms—in quarter-inch rolls with the adhesive already applied; or by the pound, in much wider rolls, without adhesive. Buy the latter if you can; it is five times cheaper. To do so, however, you must order directly from a copper supply house. The minimum order is usually 10 dollars, which is enough to last through a number of projects. The appendix lists sources for copper foil.

Because this kind of work involves a finer kind of soldering than does leaded glass, you may find it easier to work with a *soldering gun*. The Weller Temp-matic is a good one: a 150-watt gun with self-regulating heat control, which means that you won't have to keep disconnecting it, as you do your iron, to maintain a constant temperature. It costs around 13 dollars. For lampshade and jewelry operations, the chisel tip works best. We'll itemize other supplies as we go along.

Let us begin with the real thing this time. Almost every newcomer to stained-glass crafting wants to build a lampshade, and for understandable reasons. Few stained-glass products are as eyecatching, as adaptable to decor, as utilitarian, or as lovely as a shade. Gaudy or subtle, brilliant or muted, its character is capable of being altered by the simple expedient of changing from a soft to a strong bulb; or by shifting it from one part of the room to another.

Our standard precautionary comments are few. Your sense of proportion and taste should dictate the shape, color, and dimensions of your work. Keep in mind that a modern, abstract shade on a classical lamp will look bizarre; that too large or small a shade, regardless of its aesthetic merits, will look silly; and that complex and/or irregular dimensions will be quite difficult to carry off. If you are going to make a lampshade, make it essentially lampshade-shaped.

Lighting stores, antique shops, and decorator magazines are all good sources for lampshade ideas. Don't be a mere copyist, but do try to develop a specific sense of what other craftsmen have done. Haphazard experimentation will lead you eventually to a perception of the logic and balance implicit in the craft; but it is easier, and wiser, to mix innovation with imitation —at least at first. Once you have a general notion or two, do a few sketches— including in them a rough rendering of the base, too. When you hit upon a pleasing combination, develop the details of the shade to the point where you can transfer your ideas to an approximate scale drawing. You need not attempt any sophisticated drafting, unless you are up to it; translating curved surfaces to the flat plane of a sketchbook is tricky. You should be able to view on paper, however, the relative top and bottom widths, overall height, and general appearance of the lampshade before beginning actual work. If you intend to fit the shade to an existing bracket or framework, it is essential that its dimensions be taken into account at this point.

This simple scaling will also serve to indicate whether your plan involves pieces of glass too large to conform to the curved plane of the shade. Most shades are round. Because they are made of flat glass, pieces must be relatively small—depending, of course, on the overall dimensions of the shade. Your drawing will provide a rough guide as to how big you can have any one piece.

Copper foil work depends for structural rigidity on solder. (Large works in this medium also incorporate metal bracing.) Therefore, you must build your lampshade on a mold or form, which is removed only when the soldering is complete on one side. Most classical shades are bowl-shaped, and somewhere in your kitchen may be the perfect mold for your intended shade. If not, any department store carries plastic bowls in a wide variety of sizes. They are cheap enough to ruin in the process, too, which makes them a better bet than a cherished old salad bowl.

You needn't limit yourself, however, to bowl shapes. The wooden molds in the accompanying photos—one a cone, the other bell-shaped—can be duplicated on a smaller scale with papier-mâché or sculpted Styrofoam, both of which are readily available. The former can be found in any art supply shop; the latter is often carried by florists and is also used by many manufacturers for shipping purposes. Make sure that it is *Styrofoam;* other plasticized substances used for packing and insulating don't lend themselves to carving. You may not find a simple piece of Styrofoam large enough for the job, but you can easily laminate smaller pieces, bonding them with Styrofoam glue (available in art supply shops).

To make a papier-mâché mold, you can build either inside or outside an existing form. The inside of a good glass or wooden bowl, for instance, can be layered with papier-mâché mix. The resulting form will have an outside surface virtually as smooth as the inside of the original mold. If you intend to fashion your own shape from scratch, use chicken (mesh) wire, modeling it to closely approximate dimensions. Lay the mix on top of that, keeping the surface as smooth as possible. When dry, it can be further smoothed to the desired shape.

Two examples of large wooden molds used by professional craftsmen.

Little skill is required to sculpt Styrofoam. It can be carved with a sharp knife and smoothed with a rasp and sandpaper. Remember that you are fashioning a form, not a finished work of art. Therefore, be satisfied to approximate the shape.

Wooden molds are best, and if you eventually come to turn out shades in quantity and of uniform dimensions, we suggest that you have molds made up for you. For now, they are prohibitively expensive—the ones in the photos cost well over a hundred dollars each.

A small sampling of special cuts, shapes, and textures used in making lampshades.

The simplest and only sensible way to transfer your design from sketch or scale drawing to the mold, and from there, piece by piece, to the cutting stage, is to copy it freehand on the surface of the form. There are two ways to accomplish this. The best way, if you have a wooden mold, is to draw the design directly on the surface—unless you wish to preserve the mold, either to be reused or to return to the kitchen. A felt-tip pen works best.

A second method—and the one that must be used if your mold is made of papier-mâché or Styrofoam—is to cover the mold with rectangles of aluminum foil about four inches across, and draw on them. First you spray the mold with adhesive; then slap the pieces on in haphazard fashion. As long as you cover the entire mold, the application needn't be fussy. Aluminum foil, unlike papier-mâché or Styrofoam, will not melt, burn, or stick to the solder. It acts as an insulator, and also provides a reasonably smooth drawing surface.

With the design clearly delineated on the surface of the mold, number the pattern pieces. Color-key them too, if the design is complicated. Now you are ready to transfer the pattern to tracing paper—and from there, with carbon paper, to 80-pound kraft. (If you intend to use both the pattern and the mold again, as most professional craftsmen do, you'll want a precisely fitted pattern. So cut large, segmented pieces of 30-pound kraft paper, which, when fitted together, neatly join to cover the mold. An example of this can be seen in the accompanying photo. When the particular shade in process is finished, the pattern can be lifted off intact and filed away for future use.)

Using standard scissors, cut up the 80-pound kraft paper to form the actual pattern pieces for shaping the glass. Then go on to the glass cutting. Every-

Artist Franz Meyer covers his mold with a pre-cisely fitted pattern.

Cutting the pattern. Notice that standard scissors are used.

Cutting a small piece of glass.

thing we've said about this stage earlier in outlining the technique for leaded glass applies here, too. Reread that section if you have any doubts about what to do.

Once the cutting is done, the next step is to apply the copper foil to the glass pieces. If you bought a standard quarter-inch roll, you need only peel off enough to encircle each piece, allowing for a slight overlap at the joint where the two ends meet. As the photos illustrate, the foil is simply run around the edge of the glass and folded down, channel fashion, leaving an even margin of foil on either side of the edge. Because it is adhesive-backed, the rolled foil will stick neatly to the glass. After the foil is applied, burnish it down with the dull edge of a knife or a flat piece of wood such as a tongue depressor.

If you have purchased your foil by the pound in a large roll, a few additional steps are involved. To cut quarter-inch strips from large stock, first unroll a stretch about 18 inches long. Fold it over evenly into a three-layered,

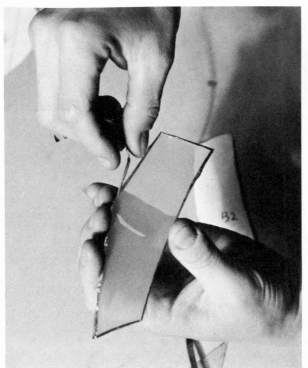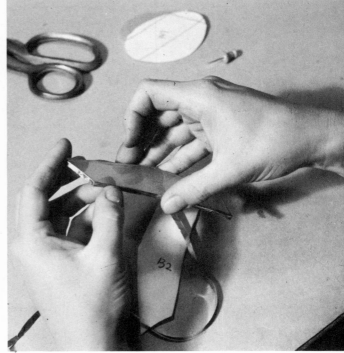

Wrapping the pieces of glass with copper foil. Allow for a slight overlap.

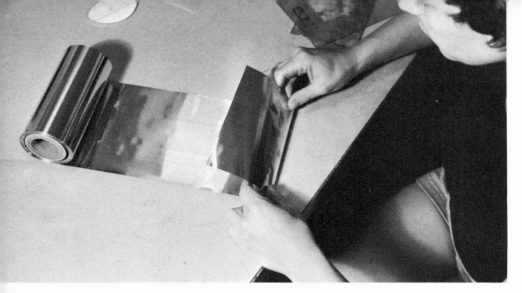

*Steps in folding
copper foil
preparatory
to cutting strips.*

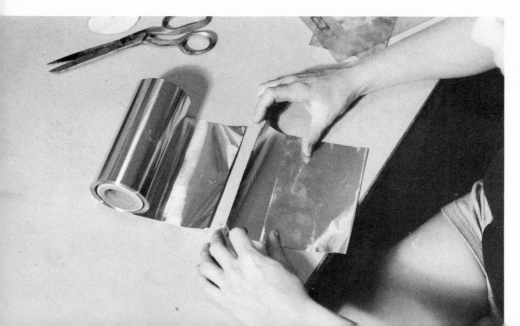

Scoring the foil with a pushpin.

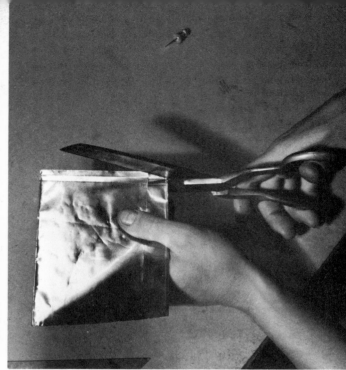

Cutting strips of foil.

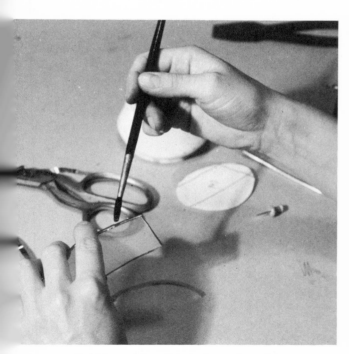

Dabbing oleic acid at the point where the copper foil is to be tacked.

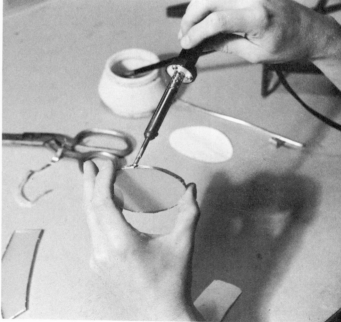

Tacking the foil with a soldering iron.

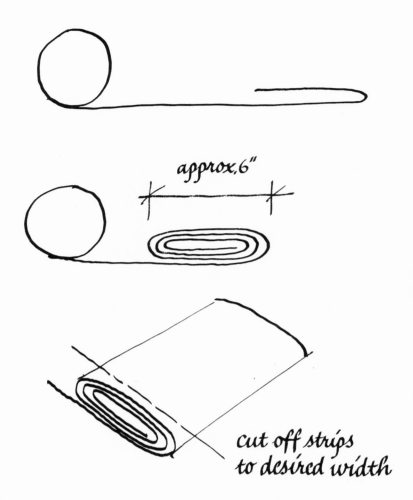

approx. 6"

cut off strips
to desired width

6-inch-long section, and mark it on the top and bottom edges at intervals of 1/4 inch. Then, using your straightedge as a guide, score the piece at each interval. A pushpin will do for this job. Now cut the foil along the score lines, using either a single-edge razor blade or standard scissors. To avoid creating a tangle of strips, don't cut more than six or so at a time. (An 18-inch strip will probably suffice for three or four pieces of glass.) Spread the strips on newspaper and spray them on one side with 3M permanent adhesive. When the application becomes tacky, the copper is ready to use.

Now you are ready to begin putting the shade together by soldering the glass into place. Use the same 60-40 solder that you used with leaded glass. Begin at the bottom edge of the construction and, because it is easier to solder on a relatively horizontal surface, tip the mold, changing the angle as you move along. Prop the first few pieces of glass in place with pushpins, touch them with oleic acid where the edges meet, and tack them together with your iron or gun. (For now, tacking is sufficient. You are merely trying to hold the pieces together for basic assembly; later you will go back and run the solder completely around the foil.) Build a full row of pieces around the base and add subsequent rows the same way, tacking as you go. Irregular patterns may not present the opportunity for working in evenly ascending rows. Try, though, not to climb too far up with one section of your design without ascending to roughly the same level with other sections. In other words, keep working *around* the mold.

With luck and patience, you will arrive at the top without incident. Time, now, to begin the full soldering job. Don't be put off by the seeming magnitude of this task; hot solder flows onto copper foil with amazing ease and speed. Try to keep the working surface as nearly horizontal as possible. Lightly coat all foil with oleic acid, and use your solder sparingly. By guiding solder and tool along the foil at a measured pace, you will find that the foil virtually coats itself. Soon the entire shade will be firmly bonded at all points.

Don't worry about gaps between the pieces. Unless you are a most exacting patternmaker and glass cutter, you are sure to leave a considerable number of holes in the work. Dribbled solder will fill the smaller ones. For bigger holes, use a filler made of bits of wadded copper foil; then dribble solder onto that. If the camouflage job is neat, no one will notice.

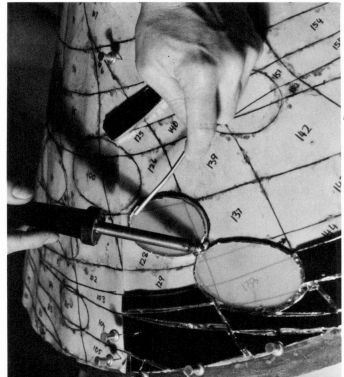

Tacking the pieces one by one on the mold. Notice the pushpins holding bottom pieces in place.

The finished lamp.

Now remove the mold and solder the inside of the shade. That done, your work will be amply rigid for its intended job.

There are two optional additional steps which more meticulous craftsmen usually perform. The first is making *floated* solder seams. These are somewhat more attractive and professional in appearance than the flat-surfaced seams we've described. Floating is difficult, however; you won't master it without practice. Before attempting it on a finished work, practice with scraps. Wrap and solder together a few pieces of glass. Then go back over the seams, keeping the soldering tool elevated about an eighth of an inch above the soldered surface. The heat of the tool will draw the solder up into a neat, uniformly convex shape—the same shape you will observe in most professional work.

The second step, not imperative but strongly advised, is the addition of a top and bottom rim. This not only adds strength; it also improves the appearance of the shade. For the bottom, 12-gauge electrical wire is ideal. It is just about the right diameter and very easy to bend. Because it is copper, it will solder readily to the foil which forms the bottom edge of the work. Your hardware dealer may not carry 12-gauge—it isn't used much anymore —but he should be able to provide an equivalent.

The rim around the top should be steel, small enough in diameter to bend handily but large enough to support any fixture to which it will in turn be soldered. To attach this top rim, we recommend the use of stainless steel flux in place of oleic acid. Available at any hardware store for about 50 cents a bottle, it helps to make an extremely strong joint. Keep it away from tools, however; it is highly corrosive. This same flux should also be used for soldering the rim to the fixture.

Don't forget, as a last step, to clean your shade of all traces of flux and incidental grime. For this, borax powder soaps and a soft brush are recommended.

You can make lampshades with standard lead channeling, too. The lead imposes obvious, somewhat severe limitations, however, and may be disappointing by comparison. For flat-sided creations, such as lanterns or

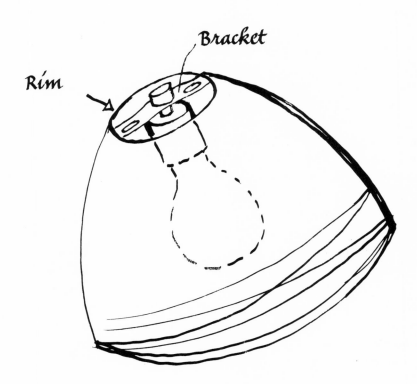

Rim

Bracket

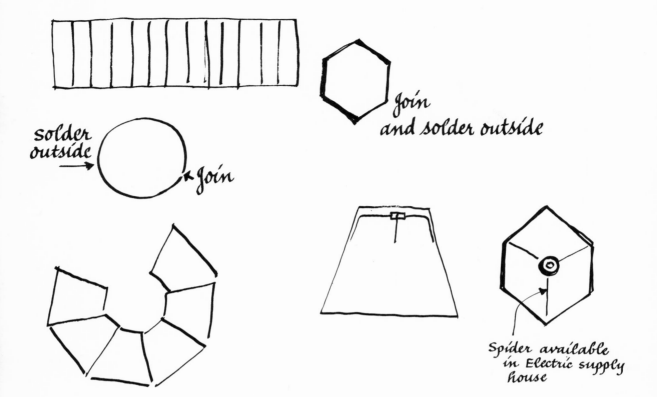

solder outside → join

join and solder outside

Spider available in Electric supply house

box lights, leaded glass is perfectly suitable. No mold is necessary; the lead itself will hold the work together during construction. Most assembly, for that matter, can be accomplished on the flat surface of your workboard. A square shade, for instance, can be first laid out, soldered on one side (the inside), and then bent slowly and carefully into a four-sided construction. Then the outside is soldered without difficulty. Or, for a simple cylindrical shade, lay out 10 to 15 strips of glass of equal size, not exceeding 3/4 inch in width. Solder them together on one side. Then round them slowly into a cylinder and solder the ends. Finally, solder the outside. Use this same procedure for making shades with any number of sides.

A slab-glass lampshade? Not impossible, but difficult. Kwick Solder, not standard solder, is the bonding agent. You will need a mold; the same one you used for your foil shade would serve. But we don't recommend making much of a pattern. It is enough to choose from your collection of scraps a variety of attractive pieces for random application. Don't select small ones, for each piece must be faceted down at the edges for a decent-looking finish. This can be a miserable, frustrating job.

Follow essentially the same directions given for building the foil shade. That is, pin the bottom pieces into place and build upward. With Kwick Solder, however, you needn't fuss about symmetry and fit; working with a spatula, you can spread it across the relatively wide spaces that this random structure will develop. To keep the Kwick Solder from sticking to the mold, use a release agent—either wax or vaseline.

What else can be done with copper foil? During the writing of this book one of our students mentioned the name of an artist in Greenwich Village. According to his report, the man was a genius in stained-glass design and had turned out marvelously imaginative creations in copper foil. Putting professional jealousy aside, we called him, partly out of curiosity and partly on the chance that he might be able to provide further ideas for the book. At his invitation we visited his studio.

One look at Ed Gilly's work was enough to convince us that our student's description was not at all exaggerated. Because he is entirely self-taught, he operates under fewer restraints than do most of us in the field. One striking result of this is a vast, undulating stained-glass bed canopy, done entirely in copper foil. It is a masterpiece. His studio is filled with master-pieces.

One of Gilly's creations is fashioned from a hubcap, another from a stove grate. A marvelous hanging shade incorporates stoplight lenses, switchboard blinker inserts, a lens from a subway signal, and a variety of other unlikely materials. Some of his work is functional, some purely decorative—such as the giant yellow butterfly in his kitchen window. Among the photos which follow this section are several taken of Gilly's creations; we offer them, and some showing the achievements of other artists in the various techniques, in place of a list of suggested projects. They seem to sum up the intended spirit of this book—that stained glass is one of the most versatile and exciting of mediums. We urge you to strike out on your own, and establish new realms of expression in glass.

A butterfly window hanging, using traditional lead and glass, executed by Felice Earley.

Two lampshades executed by Franz Meyer.

A glass-and-metal overlay executed by Jacques Duval. (Photo by John Duval)

A laminated-glass panel executed by Robert Pinart. (Photo by John Duval)

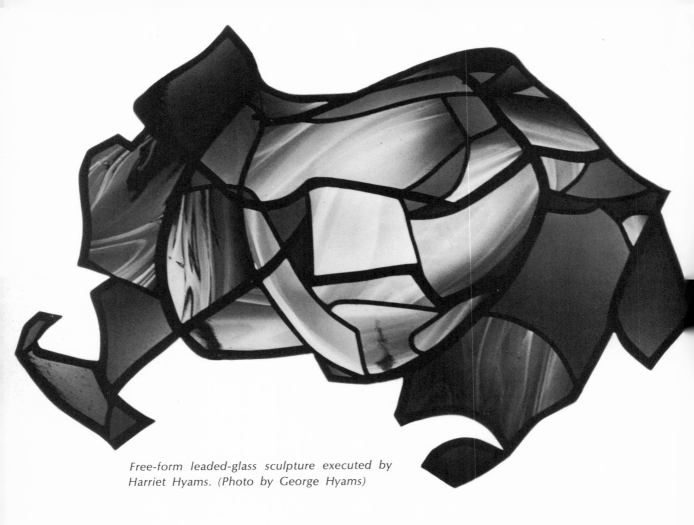

Free-form leaded-glass sculpture executed by Harriet Hyams. (Photo by George Hyams)

Laminated-glass windows executed by Harriet Hyams. (Photo by Andrew Hyams)

A small flock of leaded-glass birds executed by William J. Gerard. (Photo by William Gerard)

Two slab-glass-and-lead constructions executed by Tom Wilson. (Photo by Tom Wilson)

Three faceted pendants executed by Tom Wilson. (Photo by Tom Wilson)

Floral creations executed
by Tom Wilson.
(Photos by Tom Wilson)

Leaded-glass lanterns executed by Tom Wilson.
(Photo by Tom Wilson)

In successively closer detail, Ed Gilly's incredible bed canopy. The first view is the canopy as it appears to passersby on the street.

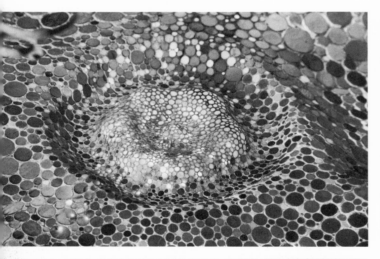

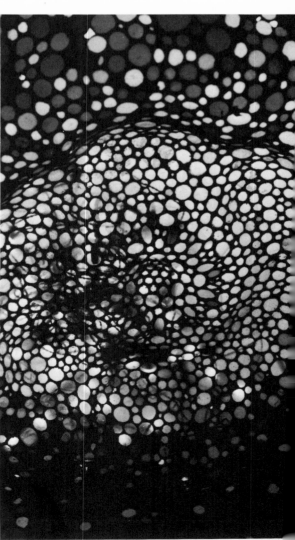

A stove grate (left) and a wall hanging in copper foil executed by Ed Gilly.

A corner of the Gilly kitchen.

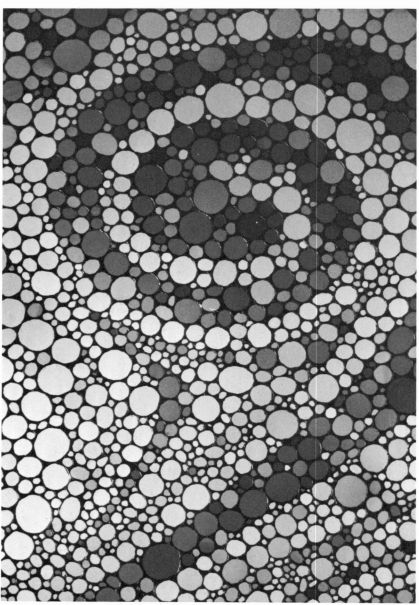

A detail of a large copper foil panel executed
by Ed Gilly.

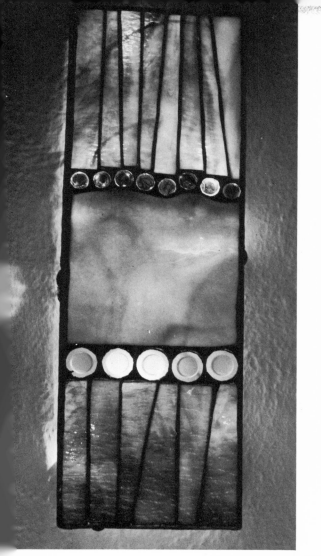

Light boxes and a hanging lamp executed by Ed Gilly.

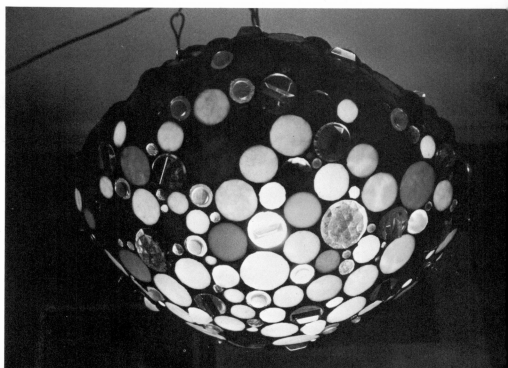

Appendix

A List of Major Suppliers

In the list below, we have given names of the major suppliers of materials required for the various techniques described in the book. Some of these companies have minimum order requirements, and it is wise to inquire as to this before ordering. Local stained-glass studios, of which there are over 400 in the country, can be very helpful in supplying small quantities of materials or in indicating other sources. The magazine *Stained Glass,* published quarterly by the Stained Glass Association of America, lists member studios and suppliers as well as giving other information about the craft. A subscription costs 5 dollars; the address is 1125 Wilmington Avenue, St. Louis, Mo. 63111.

There are two companies which can supply by mail all materials except epoxy. They are S. A. Bendheim Co., Inc., 122 Hudson Street, New York, N.Y. 10013; and Whittemore-Durgin Glass Co., Box 2065, Hanover, Mass. 02339. The latter has a very complete catalog.

Suppliers of glass:

> S. A. Bendheim Co., Inc.
> 122 Hudson Street
> New York, N.Y. 10013

> Bienenfeld Industries
> 1539 Covert Roadway
> Brooklyn, N.Y. 11227

> Blenko Glass Co.
> Milton, W. Va. 25541

> Kokomo Opalescent Glass Co.
> Box 809
> Kokomo, Ind. 46901

> The Paul Wissmach Glass Co., Inc.
> Paden City, W. Va. 26159

Suppliers of lead:

> G. A. Avril Co.
> Langdon Farm Road & Seymour Avenue
> Cincinnati, Ohio

> Crown Metal Co.
> 117 E. Washington Street
> Milwaukee, Wisc. 53204

> Gardiner Metal Co.
> 4820 S. Campbell Avenue
> Chicago, Ill. 60632

National Lead Co.
1050 State Street
Perth Amboy, N.J. 08862

White Metal Rolling & Stamping Corp.
80 Moultrie Street
Brooklyn, N.Y. 11222

Suppliers of epoxy (for casting and laminating):

Adhesive Engineering
1411 Industrial Road
San Carlos, Calif. 94070

Permagile
101 Commercial Street
Plainview, N.Y. 11803

Resin Research Co.
1989 Byberry Road
Huntingdon Valley, Penna. 19006

Thermoset Plastic Co.
5101 E. 65th Street
Box 20049
Indianapolis, Ind. 46220

Supplier of copper foil:

Conklin Brass and Copper Co., Inc.
324 W. 23rd Street
New York, N.Y. 10011

Index